PREACH THE WORD

The First Annual Peyton Lectures
Perkins School of Theology
Southern Methodist University

Preach the Word

ROY L. SMITH

ABINGDON-COKESBURY PRESS
New York · Nashville

PREACH THE WORD

COPYRIGHT MCMXLVII
BY STONE & PIERCE

K

PRINTED IN THE UNITED STATES OF AMERICA

THE PEYTON LECTURESHIP

The Peyton Lectureship on Preaching was established by Mrs. George L. Peyton, of Mexia, Texas, in memory of her husband, who was an outstanding churchman and for many years a trustee of Southern Methodist University. The lectures are to be given annually as a part of the program of Ministers' Week.

We were exceedingly fortunate in securing for the opening of this lectureship a man whose pulpit ministry has been honored of men, with the Holy Spirit himself bearing witness. Dr. Roy L. Smith was asked to prepare his messages with the idea of inspiring men to preach and showing them something of how it may be done. PREACH THE WORD is not just another volume on homiletics. The reader will be impressed with the character and quality of the material used in these lectures, but most of all he will feel that through the "foolishness of preaching" God and the Church have their best opportunity for reaching intelligent men.

The Perkins School of Theology sends forth this first series of addresses with a deep sense of gratitude to the author and to the founder of the lectureship, together with a prayer that the pulpits of the Church may possess a new power.

EUGENE B. HAWK
Dean, Perkins School of Theology

ACKNOWLEDGMENT

One of the most thrilling experiences that can come to any lecturer is that of standing before the vast audience of ministers which assembles in McFarland Auditorium on the campus of Southern Methodist University and addressing them upon some great theme related to the Christian faith. Their stimulating interest, their enthusiastic reception of the message, and the warmth of their welcome is unforgettable.

To President Umphrey Lee, of the university, and to Dean Eugene B. Hawk, of the Perkins School of Theology, I proffer sincere gratitude for the high privilege of inaugurating the Peyton Lectureship on Preaching. It stirs the imagination to anticipate the very great influence this foundation will generate in the years ahead in behalf of an effective presentation of the Christian message. Nowhere can any man speak a word in behalf of the Christian pulpit with greater hope than to those preachers of the gospel in the empire of the Southwest.

Most cordial congratulations are offered herewith to Mrs. George L. Peyton on the inspiration which launched the lectureship. The contribution which will be made in the coming years to the Christian Church through her generosity will, I am confident, be a source of much gratification to her, and serve as a crown to her great variety of benefactions. The privilege of being the first of the Peyton lecturers has been very humbling.

Roy L. Smith

CONTENTS

THE WORD

Engraved on the stone pulpit of Metropolitan Methodist Church, Detroit, Michigan, made famous by the ministry of the late Merton S. Rice, so greatly beloved throughout American Protestantism, is an unforgettable text. Carved there at his explicit direction where none but the preacher can see, it is a constant challenge to any man who stands within that pulpit and speaks to his fellow men:

Preach the Word

Horace G. Smith, president of Garrett Biblical Institute, tells the story of one of Dr. Rice's sons who was enrolled in the seminary. About every ten days or two weeks, according to President Smith, the young man received a telegram from his father. It was always the same; it never varied: "Dear Son. Preach the word. God bless you. Dad."

The words are recognized, of course, as a quotation from the Second Epistle to Timothy,[1] but their special significance derives from the circumstances under which the advice was given.

The original band of disciples who had accompanied Jesus on his travels through Galilee and Judea were all gone. With a single exception every one, if tradition is to be believed, had suffered martyrdom because of his faith in the young prophet of Galilee. There was no living person anywhere in the world who had heard the good news of salvation directly from the

11

lips of the Master. In the meantime the responsibility for leading the Christian movement had fallen upon men—many of
them young—who had received the message at second hand;
they were second-generation Christians who had been instructed in the faith by the fathers of the Church. The future
of the entire enterprise depended upon the faithfulness with
which they discharged their responsibilities, and the purity of
the faith depended upon the fidelity with which they preached
the essential truths which had come down to them from Christ
through the first-generation preachers.

It was common knowledge among the Christians that upon
the imprisonment of the Apostle Paul the responsibility for
pastoring a cluster of Christian churches had fallen upon the
shoulders of Timothy, one of the prisoner's companions in the
missionary work. This young man was a second-generation
Christian who had never had any personal contact with Jesus
except through Paul, his spiritual father. In that respect his
relationship to the movement was typical of all the preachers
of the second generation. It was for the guidance of such
young men that the Second Epistle to Timothy was written.
Regardless of who the author of the book may have been, his
advice is aimed at men who had inherited their faith, who had
received it at second hand.

Now it happened just at that time that a very great many
Greeks were coming into the Christian Church, attracted by
the exalted spirituality of the Christian message and the sublime mystery of the resurrection of Jesus. They were for the
most part honest and sincere seekers after the truth, but they
brought with them into the Church their pagan backgrounds.
Having been schooled at least in some degree in the learning
and culture of the Greek world, they found it impossible to

12

leave all their pagan concepts behind them, with the result that devout and discerning Christian thinkers, usually of the older generation, were profoundly concerned lest the Christian message should be polluted and diluted by this seepage from paganism.

All this was in the mind of the author of the Second Epistle to Timothy when he wrote to the young leaders of the Christian Church that rare bit of counsel: "Preach the word."

The godly admonition which trailed out behind the pen of that ancient Christian author sounds very simple when it falls from glib modern lips, but there is grave danger that its very simplicity may befog its seriousness and vast inclusiveness.

There are those who cite these ancient words to young preachers of today as a warning against the findings of scholars who are quarrying deep down under the surface of the Scriptures in search of their original meanings and foundations. But all such concern is the direct result of a misunderstanding of the original intent of the author. He was pleading with the young Christian pastors that they go back to the original words and teachings of Jesus and of the founding fathers. He was, in fact, pleading for scholarship.

There could be no exact or satisfactory knowledge of the original word preached by Jesus to his contemporaries in Galilee in the minds of men who were unable, or unwilling, to dig back through the accretions of paganism which had grown up about the Christian message. Some hint of what this encrustation was may be guessed from reading Colossians, Jude, and the epistles of Peter and John. The basic plea of our writer is that the Christian preachers of the second generation should go back to the original message, and in that plea the modern scholar joins with all his heart and soul.

A sermon is something different from any other form of public address. It should be logical, of course, but it must contain much more than logic. It should inform the hearer, but its function is much more than merely to teach. It should employ certain principles of psychology, but it must rise far above the mechanics of the mind. Whatever authority preaching may have will derive, not from logic, information, or psychology, but from the fact that the hearers are led to believe they are hearing from God. Even cultured listeners will forgive crudities of speech and errors in grammar if they can be convinced that they are listening to the description of a judgment from the Most High.

Following the famous debate on war at the Methodist General Conference of 1944 in Kansas City, Missouri, a distinguished layman—a judge who had voted against the position taken by Ernest Fremont Tittle—said: "That preacher makes me feel very strange. I disagree with many things he says, but he makes me feel that I am disagreeing with God, and not with him. That makes me very uncomfortable."

The advice to "preach the word" rests upon the doctrine that God has spoken to man. The word is something that has been committed to the preacher. He is not responsible for its acceptability or its implications. That is God's responsibility. The preacher's duty is to proclaim it.

This means that he must know what the word was *when it was first spoken, and what it meant to those who heard it first.*

The moment the preacher begins to dig down into his Scriptures to uncover the word he discovers that God spoke to men out of a variety of crises. Indeed there is a sense in which it may be said that the Bible is a book born of crises. Some were political, some were economic, some were social, some were international in their aspect, and some were intensely personal. One of the most impressive facts which one will meet in any serious study, of the Old Testament particularly, is that in every crisis God found some devout and fearless soul through whom he could speak to the people. Through New as well as through Old Testament writers he expressed his judgments.

This means, of course, that God's words were always contemporary. The solemn sermons with which Isaiah warned the kingdom of Judah throughout the last half of the eighth century B.C. were preached to a nation which was staggering from one political and international crisis to another. If the judgments of God were true in those fateful days, as we most firmly believe they were, then they were also true in other similar crises that followed, and they will be found to be true in our day when the same circumstances prevail. To understand God's judgments, however, we must know with some exactness the circumstances under which they were uttered.

When we attempt to approach the Scriptures from this viewpoint, we make the discovery that the word is not the simple thing it is sometimes made to sound on the lips of certain uninformed advisers of preachers. It is as complex and variegated as life itself, for it was born of life. In its original form it was spoken to collaborationists, traitors, exploiters, appeasers, traducers, seducers, grafters, dollar diplomats, power politicians, connivers, reactionaries, and borers-from-within. It was also spoken to heroes, saints, crusaders, reformers, social engineers, and faithful preachers of righteousness. It was a word that had to do with public morals, social abuses, and political perfidy; and it was a word that had to do with private vices, personal religion, and the individual's relationship with God.

The stories of this book are an effort to re-create some of the scenes which must have been enacted when the word was first spoken to men. To understand the passion with which it was charged we must feel the seriousness of the crises amid which it was born. Once we have known the great souls to whom it was entrusted we shall be better able to "preach the word" to the people and for the circumstances of our own day. If, from some point of vantage, we can look in upon the heroic spirits to whom God committed his judgments, and watch them as they struggled with the issues with which they were confronted, we begin to discover the glory and the majesty of the word which was given to them, and which they in turn have handed down to us.

As we watch the shifting scene out of which the word emerged, stretching down through many centuries, we suddenly discover that it is a living, pulsing thing which embraces all of life. Far from being a mysterious word which speaks of incomprehensible apocalypses, it is a vivid, blazing word which runs clear out to the uttermost horizons of experience. There is no interest or motive of life where it is not heard; nothing that has to do with the enrichment or the impoverishment of life is outside its implications. The word we are called to preach is a message of redemption of all of life for all men.

The word which the Christian preacher finds within his Scriptures, and which he is admonished to preach, is not the fruitage of a single mind, nor is it a judgment related to a single theme. It is rather, as some imaginative soul has said, "like the multi-colored light that streams in through some magnificent stained-glass window, each little fragment of which has contributed its hue to the glorious whole." Prophets of righteousness and justice have contributed the flaming reds and yellows; patient scholars have added the more sober purples and blues; sweet-spirited psalmists, with the souls of poets, have inserted many a pastel shade; martyrs and the crucified have tinged it here and there with the deep crimson of blood; sturdy believers who "mocked the cross and flame" have lent their clear ultramarines and greens. The result is a spiritual mosaic of transcendent loveliness, the wonder and meaning of which no mind can ever exhaust.

The fundamental task of the good minister of Jesus Christ is to interpret to modern men the word of God spoken aforetime to sensitive souls. This means that he must think again with the minds of men long gone, and feel again with their sensitivity. He must stand where they stood, experience their indignations and compassions, and turn as they did to divine fountains for faith and courage. Above all he must remember that the word he preaches is not his own; it has been given to him from the heart of the Eternal.

the Word... OF THE PROPHETS

I

The Education of Jesus

Boyish voices, high pitched and lusty, filled the little Nazareth synagogue as a score or more of youngsters seated in a circle about the room, facing the old rabbi, droned out their lessons in the ancient Law and Prophets of Israel. Peering out from under snowy white brows, the beady black eyes of the aged man moved deliberately along the line, taking careful note of every lad. Not a detail of either interest or conduct escaped his attention. Schooling was serious business in Nazareth under Rabbi ben Ispah of the School of Hillel.

The spirit of democracy had always been strong among the Jews of Galilee, but even the most impartial masters have their favorites, and, in spite of his determination to be just, the eye of the venerable ben Ispah paused now and again to study the beautiful face and to listen appreciatively to the sweet voice of a certain twelve-year-old who sat almost directly in front of him. There was a strange light in the boy's eyes as he intoned the majestic and sonorous phrases of the ancient prophets, as if they kindled deep fires within his being. It was very evident that he was one of those rare spirits with whom learning is a passion.

It was only a few days before that the lad had created something of a sensation in the Jerusalem temple by entering into a discussion of delicate matters of the Law with some learned doctors.[2] His familiarity with the teachings of the prophets and his amazing mastery of the intricacies of the Law had astounded them. Never had they heard such words from the lips of a child, and even the wisest of them marveled.

"Who is he?"

"By whom has he been taught?"

"Does he know these things of himself, or has the spirit of prophecy been laid upon him?"

"Who is his father, and who is his mother?"

Such were the questions that ran through the crowd which listened to his conversation with the doctors, and no one seemed able to answer beyond the simple fact that he was the son of a carpenter from Nazareth.

The whole affair had created a small furor in Jerusalem and no end of gossip in Nazareth. Women passed the word back and forth through the village, and men discussed it in the market place. Meanwhile, at least some part of the glory was reflected upon the good name of the aged Rabbi ben Ispah, for was it not he who had schooled the lad in the sacred lore of Israel? As the old man furtively studied the expressive features of this fascinating boy in the little Nazareth synagogue, however, he was compelled to admit within his own heart that there was something beyond the understanding of any man. He could not explain it, even to himself, but he knew that he was dealing with a soul that had somehow sensed the holy presence of the Divine.

In the meantime it was ben Ispah's duty to see that the youngsters kept on with their studies. The stern discipline of many years in the synagogue forbade that he should allow a sensation in the Jerusalem temple to disturb the routine of his little school. Even if there was an eagle in his flock, that would not justify any neglect of the others who might be no more than plain barnyard fowls. Were not they all born in the image of the same God?

The white-haired old rabbi pulled himself together with a start and cast his eyes over his school once again. Such moments of abstraction as the one in which he had just indulged himself might prove disastrous, even though nothing had happened this time. Every boy was intent upon his studies, droning out the familiar passages and swaying rhythmically with his body as he recited the ponderous lines, but through the din ben Ispah was always dimly conscious of the intonations of the carpenter's son in his rich young soprano voice.

"Holy, holy, holy, is the Lord of hosts: the whole earth is full of his glory." [3]

"He hath showed thee, O man, what is good; and what doth the Lord require of thee, but to do justly, and to love mercy, and to walk humbly with thy God?" [4]

"Seek good, and not evil, that ye may live: and so the Lord, the God of hosts, shall be with you, as ye have spoken." [5]

"I hate, I despise your feast days, and I will not smell in your solemn assemblies. Though ye offer me burnt offerings and your meat offerings, I will not accept them: neither will I regard the peace offerings of your fat beasts. Take thou away from me the noise of thy songs; for I will not hear the melody of thy viols. But let judgment run down as waters, and righteousness as a mighty stream." [6]

"He is despised and rejected of men; a man of sorrows, and acquainted with grief: and we hid as it were our faces from him; he was despised, and we esteemed him not. Surely he hath borne our griefs, and carried our sorrows: yet we did esteem him stricken, smitten of God, and afflicted. But he was wounded for our transgressions, he was bruised for our iniquities: the chastisement of our peace was upon him; and with his stripes we are healed." [7]

On and on the boy went, the mighty words of the ancient men of God pouring from his lips in a veritable stream. Never was the sonorous speech of the Jews more beautiful than that morning when it was chanted in the clear boyish voice uttering the noble faith of the prophets. The fiery invective of Amos, the cultured liberalism of Isaiah, the infinite tenderness of Hosea, the haunting pathos of Jeremiah, so strangely sad, the flaming faith of the prophet of the Exile—it all seemed like the breath of life to the carpenter's son. In it his mind was steeped; on it his soul had fed from the earliest days of understanding. It was the language of his spiritual homeland.

As he looked out through the latticed window of the synagogue toward the mountains, he seemed to be living in the same world with the prophets whose solemn words he had been repeating. Then as he gazed with a far-off expression on his face, in his imagination the figure of the prophet Elijah came striding down from the mountains of Gilead to cry out again in condemnation of a king who had despoiled a peasant. A flash of recognition lighted up the lad's eyes, for it was with the thunderous protest of the Gileadite that the stream of Hebrew prophecy had really taken its rise, and at this stream the carpenter's son had been drinking all his years.

II
The Beginning of the Word

Naboth was in trouble!

Far back in the shadowy days when the Hebrews were first getting a foothold in the Land of Promise—hundreds of years before—the founder of Naboth's family had settled upon a little tract of land not many miles from Nazareth, and had been confirmed in his title thereto by the elders of the clan. All generations of Nabothians since that time had tilled its soil and drawn their living from its generosity.

Now to Hebrews ownership of the land was something sacred. From the soil they had their livelihood. It was God who had given it fertility; it was God who had given it to their fathers; it was God who had vouched for its title by the terms of the Covenant sealed and vowed in the wilderness. Other races of men might buy and sell the land, but not so a son of Abraham. To him the soil was a symbol of stability. Preserving one's patrimony intact and inviolate was one of the fundamentals of "the Hebrew way." To sell one's heritage, or to allow it to pass out of one's possession, was to repudiate everything sacred and alienate oneself from God and the nation. It was equivalent to becoming a renegade and a vagabond. The little farm upon which Naboth lived was to him the emblem of all things holy—faith, patriotism, morality, family name, personal honor. It was his credential as a citizen and the guaranty of his status as a freeman and an elder of Israel.

But life had been changing of late. The foundations of everything Hebrew had been shaken. Ancient standards were breaking up before men's eyes. Ahab, the king, had married Jezebel, a daughter of Ethbaal, the king of Tyre and a pagan

23

priest; and though the marriage was not the cause of the social revolution, it was at least a symptom.

Israel was passing through a major economic and political crisis. Omri, Ahab's father, in a remarkable reign which had extended through almost half a century, had unified the nation, developed its internal resources, and fortified its borders. But nowhere along its coast was there anything resembling a bay wherein seagoing ships might come to harbor, with the result that the mounting stores of Hebrew grain were at the mercy of the traders of Tyre. Those shrewd merchants, well aware of the advantages of their position, took full liberties with the bottleneck across which they lived and levied exorbitant tribute against the helpless Hebrew farmers, growing enormously rich in the process. In an effort to break the iron ring with which his little kingdom was surrounded, Omri had manipulated the marriage of his son Ahab to Ethbaal's daughter Jezebel, and by that means he had opened up the Tyrian markets to Hebrew produce.

At first it had appeared to be smart statesmanship. Prices took a sharp upswing, the farmers began to enjoy an unprecedented prosperity, and new luxury goods appeared in the bazaars of Samaria, Dan, Bethel, and Shechem. The merchants of the kingdom were especially pleased and extolled the genius of Omri and his son Ahab, proclaiming them the saviors of the nation.

But something besides money began to inundate the land. Strange priests appeared on the streets of the capital, imported by Queen Jezebel from the temples of Tyre, and with the alien priests came also alien ideas of economics and politics.

Between the sanctities of Israel and Tyre there was all the difference there is between right and wrong, east and west, up and down. Whereas, in Hebrew thinking, the land was invested with sanctity, to the Tyrian it was nothing more than another bit of merchandise to be bought or sold as one's whim or pleasure might dictate. Among the Tyrians no man enjoyed any rights except those granted him by his monarch, and these were at all times at the mercy of imperial caprice. But among the Hebrews each individual citizen was guaranteed rights because he was born a Hebrew—a child of the Covenant.

Foremost among those ancient Hebrew rights was the inviolability of the freeman's title to his land. A heritage such as that of Naboth's was protected against even the cupidity of a monarch. It had been as secure as a modern man's rights of trial by jury, and no king had ever before dared violate the holdings of a humble and defenseless citizen. It was for this reason that the Naboth case became the hinge by which the floodgates were opened and paganism in all its brazen disregard of the rights of the individual swept in upon the nation.

Ahab, the king, wanted the patrimony of Naboth, the farmer.[8] He proposed to add it to the royal estate and was perfectly willing to pay for it. Indeed, he would pay well— far more than the land was worth—and if this was unsatisfactory he was willing to arrange an exchange whereby Naboth might become the owner of a larger and more valuable farm somewhere else in the kingdom. According to modern business ethics there was nothing about the king's proposition that would subject it to criticism. It was not a case of robbery. Rather, it was a good real-estate deal in which the farmer might make a neat profit if he bargained with skill.

But it would be at the expense of everything Naboth held sacred!

The farmer's stubbornness was a puzzle to Jezebel. The

queen was altogether unable to understand either the reluctance of Naboth or the caution of Ahab. Had a similar situation arisen in her father's kingdom, the ruthless old Ethbaal, onetime priest of Baal, would have driven the peasant off his land without a twinge of conscience and would have counted himself foolishly lenient because he did not kill the recalcitrant as an example to any others who might become infected with the poison of independence. Had he done so, not one voice in all the realm would have been raised in protest because no one in Tyre would have sensed anything wrong in the brutality of the king. Baalism did not concern itself with the rights of humble men in the ownership of their land.

Looking back upon the scene from the vantage point of the twentieth century of Christian civilization, we may easily see that every man living today had a definite stake in the outcome of the Naboth case. The issue was terribly simple. Stripped of all ancient formulas it was this: *Does the individual have rights which the state is bound to respect?*

To Jezebel, reared according to the pagan philosophy of Baalism, such a concept of life and morals was intolerable, not to say ridiculous. Of what value would a crown be if a king's rule was not absolute? What was the state if it was not to be supreme and unquestioned? What would become of government if monarchs were required to give way to peasants? What were civil rights that they should conflict with the desires of royalty?

It is easy to imagine the scene enacted within the royal palace the day Ahab came back to his queen, fretting over the obstinate refusal of Naboth to sell. The king knew full well the ancient and substantial basis for the farmer's unwillingness, and he was too much a Hebrew to ignore it. Indeed, the struggle within his own soul was terrible, with conviction holding out against the seduction of cupidity. Jezebel, on the other hand, was bewildered and indignant.

"But you are the king, are you not?" she demanded, angrily. "Who is this nobody that would refuse my lord's desire?"

"Yea, it is true, I am the king," Ahab answered, avoiding her blazing eyes. "But among the Hebrews there is an ancient law and custom, sealed by the Covenant with our God in the wilderness, and no man, even though he be a king, may transgress that law." Though he spoke the truth, he neither succeeded in convincing his queen nor in fortifying his own spirit. The pagan soul of Jezebel was completely immunized against all appeals of mercy or justice, for that is the inevitable result of paganism.

Aware at last that she could not persuade Ahab to act with forthrightness, Jezebel took matters into her own hands. With utter callousness she contrived the death of the faithful freeman and cleared the way for the exercise of the royal whim.

With Naboth safely dead and Ahab in possession of his patrimony, the nation was exposed to Baalism and its pagan philosophy of land ownership. That meant an utter indifference toward all rights of individual citizens when those rights conflicted with the power of the state. In that hour politics, economics, and statesmanship were all dumb, because they knew nothing more holy than expediency. Slaves of the state, they justified all royal ruthlessness on the grounds of profit or advantage.

But there was one other voice in Israel that day—*the voice of religion*. When everything else bowed in submission, and while the blood of freemen cried out from the ground, the prophet of God summoned the state to judgment.

Comparatively little is known concerning Elijah the Tishbite, beyond the simple fact that he came down out of the mountains of Gilead from time to time, a heroic figure with the stamp of the desert upon his body and mind. Thundering the judgments of God, he was the ancient conscience of Israel incarnate. To him the sanctities of life were still sacred. The principles upon which the nation's faith was built were still valid. Jehovah, the God of Israel, was still in authority, and the ancient Covenant, sealed with great solemnity in the wilderness by their fathers, was still in force.

It was not that Ahab proposed to dispense with religion. Not at all. It is probably true that there was more religion in Samaria the day Naboth died than ever before in the history of Israel, *but it was religion without a social conscience or any sense of morals*. Ahab was a perfect personification of the state; he had no quarrel with religion until it began passing judgments.

It is quite possible that Ahab went directly to the shrine with Naboth's blood still dripping from his hands, for despoilers of men and debauchers of public morals were as welcome at the "high places" as honest and God-fearing men, so long as they were willing to add sacrifices to the pile of carcasses on the blazing pyre, and join in the rhythmic and often obscene chants around the altar. It was a comfortable religion that charged itself with no responsibility for public or private morals, and required no social concern of its devotees.

Into such a system Elijah did not fit, for his majestic convictions, born of the Spirit of the Lord whom he had met among the mountains of Gilead, made him an angular prophet who could not move comfortably in a world that satisfied itself with ritual and unmorality.

The story, as it was told to the carpenter's son, first by his mother and then by the venerable Rabbi ben Ispah, was fragmentary and lacked many details, but it fired the soul of the growing lad, even as it stirs our imagination to this day. It would be easy to follow our fancy into fascinating bypaths and reconstruct some of the searching questions with which the boy Jesus plied his old teacher. Mary's Magnificat tempts us to believe that the fires of social protest burned deep within her heart,[9] and who knows how much of Jesus' compassion for the poor was the product of her oneness with the lowly? But anyone who heard him speak during the years of his ministry in Galilee could not fail to detect the echoes of the voice of Elijah in his preaching.

It is not within our province to trace the history of prophecy in detail, but the Christian preacher is entirely within his rights in declaring that nowhere among all the records of men are there to be found such unequivocating declarations of the sanctity of human rights as in the sermons of the Hebrew prophets, and the stream of that mighty tide can be said to have begun with Elijah the Tishbite. From his day onward no Hebrew king was ever free from the threat of a prophetic judgment if he dared to launch out upon a career of injustice or ungodliness. Something about the way the prophets proclaimed their judgments convinced the people, and even the kings, that they spoke for God.

Whole libraries have been written about them and their sermons, and their every extant word has been dissected with meticulous care to discover within it the last possible shred of meaning. The result is that the prophets are both the best understood and the most misrepresented individuals who have come down to us from ancient times.

It is not our purpose to study the way they have been mistakenly masqueraded by their pseudo friends as men of mystery who predicted the modern world with all its miracles and confusion. We must be content to view them as preachers with a consuming social passion, an independent moral judgment, and a profound belief that they were divinely commissioned to preach the judgments of God. It is their preaching which provides the moral and social seedbed that nourishes modern Christian preaching.

III

Six Facts Explaining the Prophets

Even the casual student of the four Gospels must be impressed by the way Jesus turned to the Old Testament prophets for inspiration and guidance. On their sermons he had been reared. Those lessons, learned so thoroughly in the little synagogue school, colored much of what he said when, as a preacher hailed as the prophet of Galilee, he proclaimed the beginning of the kingdom of heaven. His sermons bore the ineradicable mark of their social, moral, and spiritual pioneering. There can be no explanation of his utterances, or of the preaching of the Christian Church down through the centuries, which ignores the preaching of the prophets. He who would preach the word must know the prophets, and six facts about them.

1. *They were men of their times.* Each was immersed in his own generation; each offered a solution for some social, political, economic, moral, or religious situation that threatened the soul of the nation of which he was an immediate

part; each had a personal stake in the nation's choice of policy and threw all the powers of his being into the effort to persuade the nation to act righteously.

Amos was one of the poorest of the shepherds of Judah, who suffered with others exploited like himself. Micah was a countryman who watched his fellow villagers writhe under the oppressions of money-grabbing landlords. Hosea's home had been broken up by the slimy corruption of a sex-obsessed paganism which erupted over the land. Jeremiah was a small landowner of Anathoth whose family fortune was involved in the stability of the nation. Isaiah was as closely identified with the political crises of Judah through the last half of the seventh century B.C. as H. G. Wells was with the affairs of the British Empire during the last generation.

Self-styled teachers of prophecy who attempt to wrench the prophets out of their native land and century, compelling them to predict the events of this morning's headlines, are as fundamentally false to them as though they should deny that they ever existed. The prophets were men of their own day who saw God at work in their own generation upon problems which made life unbearable for their contemporaries. Out of their experiences among their countrymen they came forward with a word which they declared was from God. Because they spoke that divine word to their own age, they are worthy of a hearing now, for truth is at home in any century.

Prophetic preaching, therefore, is contemporaneous preaching—neither behind its generation nor ahead of its time. It is a proclamation of the judgments of God upon the passing scene, a cry for justice above "good politics," a warning that the universe is still under the authority of a moral order, a

31

stalwart defense of the rights of the individual. The credential of prophetic preaching is not its acceptance by any group, class, or philosophy; the vital fact is its divine endorsement.

2. *They were men of the people.* It is very interesting to discover that only two of the long list of those whose sermons are preserved for us in the Old Testament were in any sense members of a class that could be called professionally religious. Nahum seems to have been a prophet connected in some way with the services of the temple in Jerusalem. Ezekiel was a priest who was carried away from Jerusalem in the first of Nebuchadrezzar's deportations (597 B.C.). All the others were laymen without professional affiliations or peculiar prophetic training, who represented neither a class nor an economic bloc. They asked nothing for themselves; they aspired to no office; they headed no revolt; they led no party dedicated to any political theory. It is true that protests did develop among the people as a result of the preaching of some of them, but the prophets themselves were in no sense partisans. Theirs was the power of independence, for they held aloof from all partisanship and proclaimed the judgments of God with complete impartiality.

The full significance of the prophetic message will be missed if we do not keep in mind the fact that the prophets lived through a period marked by a class struggle which was both bitter and prolonged. The cleavage between the city capitalists and the country gentry threatened the very life of the nation on more than one occasion. Hints of the seriousness of the conflict appear here and there in Isaiah [10] and Jeremiah,[11] but they come out boldly in Amos [12] and Micah.[13] Strong-arm men, gangsters, the Gestapo, ruffians, and mercenaries slink through the shadows like evil spirits. The depressed and exploited classes—the "people of the land"—fight through one generation after another in a desperate effort to achieve even a few of the common rights of life.

From such a struggle the prophets could not possibly hold aloof, and their sermons are redolent with the spirit of protest. Always they plead for simple justice. Their sympathies are always with the sufferers, but their consciences are always sensitive to sin, even though it be the sufferers who are sinning.

Prophetic preaching, therefore, is popular preaching—preaching in behalf of the people. It espouses causes, not classes; it pleads for principles, not for parties. And that kind of preaching often makes it necessary for the preacher to stand out against the crowd itself in order to be true to the crowd.

3. *They were the real patriots of their day.* Sin was almost exclusively a social phenomenon among the Hebrews as a result of the sealing of the Covenant with Jehovah in the wilderness. By that compact, which was to them all that the Constitution is to the modern American, the nation was guaranteed the aid and blessing of God. Any individual who violated the terms of the Covenant delayed the divine blessing, and to that extent became a traitor to the nation. Every Hebrew prospered or suffered according to the way in which the nation prospered or suffered. There was no salvation independent of national salvation. It was not until Jeremiah's time that anyone—priest, prophet, king, or private citizen—thought of sin as anything that affected personal fortunes or destiny apart from the nation's fortunes or destiny. The result was that righteousness and patriotism were almost entirely synonymous.

According to the terms of the Covenant, national salvation

depended upon national righteousness, and it became, therefore, a matter of primary importance that there should be a clear and definite concept of the exact meaning of righteousness. There dare not be any mistake in the matter, and yet it was precisely on that sector that the prophets' war was waged through almost three hundred years.

According to the popular theology of the day, which was taught by priests and professional prophets, righteousness consisted of the performance of stated ceremonies, offering adequate sacrifices, burning proper incense, and observing new moons and assemblies punctiliously. All this was little better than holy magic, completely devoid of any moral significance, and against it the prophets protested mightily. Righteousness to them had little to do with ceremonies.[14] Instead, it consisted of social justice,[15] efficiency and honesty in public office, an equitable administration of law in behalf of all the people, an undeviating loyalty to Jehovah, and unimpeachable morals both public and private.

Because the prophets loved their nation with a consuming passion, they gave their utmost to establish righteousness. Anything, in their opinion, which was for the good of the people had the approval of God, and they therefore worked for it with all their powers. Anything that did not benefit the people was under the condemnation of God, and by the same token they fought it with all their energies. For this reason none of them were ever able to keep out of politics, and none ever drew a line between the sacred and the secular. Such devotion to the people established them as the most exalted patriots of their time, even though they were, for the most of the time, in conflict with the ruling powers of the state.

Prophetic preaching, therefore, will be patriotic. It will

view life as a whole, not as a series of compartmentalized interests, never attempting to distinguish between the sacred and the secular. Anything that enriches life is sacred, and anything that impoverishes life is sinful and therefore to be condemned. The true prophet will not hesitate to invade any field—social, economic, or political—if the forces from that field are befouling the life of the people.

4. *They claimed divine authority for their utterances.* Here it is necessary to speak of the prophets and their preaching with the greatest of care lest we seem to sanction many wild fancies now current. The prophets themselves give only the vaguest hints as to the exact processes—psychological, intellectual, or spiritual—by which they came into possession of their messages. True, Isaiah makes a rather extended reference to a vision that came to him in the temple,[16] and Ezekiel reports that he occasionally experienced some sort of seizures.[17] But these are the exception, and in neither case do they explain what the prophets had to say. We get the impression, however, that the prophets were godly men, profoundly pious, to whom the judgments of God were supremely precious. We know from our own experience that such devotion produces spiritual sensitivity, and we can believe that the prophets became so sensitive to the impact of the Holy Spirit of the living God that they heard things from him that are not given to ordinary men. There is no question about their confidence that their message came from God.

Without a single exception the preaching of the prophets produced a profound impression. Ahab trembled when he looked into the blazing eyes of Elijah and cried out, "Hast thou found me, O mine enemy?" It would have been easier to face the spears of an army of invading Assyrians than to

35

look into the depths of the prophet's eyes. Ahaz, frantically preparing to defend Jerusalem against Pekah and Rezin, was unable to answer the measured words of Isaiah; [18] and Amaziah, the presiding priest at Bethel, was thrown into a panic by Amos' sermon even though he knew he had Jeroboam's armies at his back.[19]

But this conviction of divine sanction produced an even greater impression on the prophets themselves. Under its influence they stood out against kings as they would not have dared to do if they had been armed only with swords and spears and had been dependent entirely upon their own strength. They became men of amazing courage who thrust themselves into the royal presence of rulers and delivered their souls without fear or favor. Nowhere else in all the world were there those who would have dared attempt such behavior, and it is a part of the glory of the Hebrew people that such conduct became something of a commonplace among them.

Prophetic preaching, therefore, will rely for its power upon divine sanction. The prophets would never have dared speak as they did if they had not believed they were speaking for God and not for themselves. The sanctity of their message provided immunity for their persons. Let the modern preacher who presumes to speak prophetically be sure of this same divine authority and endorsement.

5. *They dealt with great moral principles.* Generally contemptuous toward the formalities of religion, the prophets allied morality with faith. Their teachings were extremely simple, so simple indeed that they sound almost axiomatic to modern ears. But we must never allow ourselves to forget that we are studying men who lived at the dawn of history,

when the race was just coming up to the level of political consciousness and morality.

Injustices, they said, will wreck a nation. Evil will destroy any people. God and righteousness will ultimately triumph in this world. No ally of God's need ever fear. Individuals have a sanctity which must be respected because all men are born in the image of God.

Simple? Yes! Primitive? Of course! Elemental? Certainly! But so also was the wheel, the lever, and the stone which a boy swung in his sling for the first time. Yet every laborer who lays his burden upon a wheel, and every worker who watches a lever lifting his load, is indebted to those primitive men who pioneered with the principles. We have made many different wheels since that first one, but we have never improved upon the principle which was discovered in the first wheel. We have devised many governments since Elijah's time, but we have never improved upon the moral principles he defended that day in the court of King Ahab. And who, for that matter, has ever described in plainer language the duty of a righteous man than did Micah the Morashtite? Or who has ever given governments and kings better advice than did the rustic shepherd of Tekoa as he cried out against social and political sins at the Bethel shrine?

Prophetic preaching, therefore, will deal with great moral principles and allow the judgments to fall where they may, whether on money lord or on labor leader. It will warn the nation by every device at its command that evil carries within itself the seeds of its own destruction, and then identify evil wherever it lifts its ugly face. That such preaching calls for great courage and rare discrimination is perfectly true, but he who aspires to preach the word must be willing to pay the price of preparation that will enable him thus to discriminate courageously.

6. *They were always in the minority.* It is a fact which deserves the most deliberate consideration that the prophets always walked alone. The ministry of the true prophet is at all times a lonely business. Only once in all the turbulent half century through which he preached did Isaiah enjoy the confidence of his monarch to the point that he was called in for counsel in affairs of state.[20] The prophetic party which he organized for the purpose of perpetuating his ideas was compelled to go underground soon after his death. Not one of the great prophets of the eighth and seventh centuries B.C. ever had the thrill of seeing his ideas put into practical effect. With the single exception of Nahum, who lived to rejoice in the downfall of Nineveh, the prophets of both those tragic centuries lived lives crammed with disappointments and discouragements. Such is apt to be the experience of true prophets in all generations, for faith always walks ahead of experience.

Prophetic preaching, therefore, may accept welcome applause but must not be deflected by it. Truth never depends upon a plebiscite, and the preacher of truth is never deterred by the fact that he is numbered with the few. At the same time, the prophetic preacher will not be deluded into thinking that persecution is the mark of perfection, nor that loneliness is a guaranty that he has read the mind of God aright. It sometimes happens that God is also with the majority.

IV

Four Characteristics of the Prophetic Word

Let the modern preacher, advised to "preach the word," turn again to the word of the prophets. Let him examine his own foundations with the utmost care. Let him steep his mind and soul in the sermons of those just men upon whose ideas the mind of the Master was fed. Let him watch Amos at Bethel and Jesus cleansing the temple. Let him quiet his soul and, with the Old Testament open before him, let him hear the wistful cry of Hosea as he weeps over Israel, saying, "O Ephraim!" [21] Then let him turn to his New Testament and hear the Master sob, "O Jerusalem!" [22] Let him compare Jesus and Jeremiah and note their similarities. Reading the New Testament against a frieze of the prophets will reveal a succession of instances in which the ancient preachers spoke again through the Prophet of Galilee, whose mind, as a child, was piloted through their majestic ideas by the venerable rabbi in the Nazareth synagogue.

1. *The prophetic word expressed the mind of God with a certain magnificent indifference.* The professional prophets might rant and rave, they might rush violently to the defense of the *status quo,* they might connive with the politicians to throw the true prophets into the dungeons; but even death to those fearless preachers was only an incident and held no terrors. Popular acclaim or flying stones, personal danger or royal threats, loneliness, betrayal, torture—none of these things moved them, for they had meat to eat of which the crowds knew nothing. Theirs was the glory of living for a single purpose—to do the will of God and to proclaim that will unto all the sons of men.

2. *The prophetic word was clear thinking about sin.* Brushing aside the magic and mummery of the shrines, and putting their fingers squarely upon the open sores of the body politic, the prophets identified sin with personal as well as with collective conduct. No preacher in the twentieth century who is

not capable of straight thinking on this subject can hope to assist in the world's redemption. We may better be vague about our sociology and our economics than suffer from any illusions concerning the tragedy of sin within the human soul.

3. *The prophetic word summoned men to hear the judgments of God.* The Hebrew preachers never allowed the Hebrew nation to forget that it was dealing with God. In every crisis, in the face of every decision, some spokesman for God arose to say, "Thus saith the Lord." In Ezekiel's figure of the watchman upon the wall [23] we catch a glimpse of their holy succession crying out and warning the nation against the awful fate that awaits any people or any individual who violates the laws of God. Such preaching is neither comforting nor comfortable; but, like the surgeon's knife that cuts away diseased tissue, it is sometimes the only thing that can save a generation. Imagine, if you can, an engineer who would ignore the law of gravity, or a chemist who would ignore the law of chemical affinity, or a nation that would ignore the moral laws of God. There is something much more serious than a fine phrase in the prophetic warning from the Psalms which the carpenter's son learned in the schoolroom of the little Nazareth synagogue: *"The way of the ungodly shall perish."* [24] It cannot be otherwise in a universe that expresses the moral integrity of God, and every nation needs to be warned again and again against the dangers of defiance.

4. *The prophetic word declared an unshaken faith in the justice of God.* Ours is no absentee God waiting on plebiscites, but an active personal presence vigorously at work in the affairs of men, whose ultimate glory and victory are inevitable because he is God. Gone are the tyrants of yesteryear whose doom the Hebrew prophets foretold, and likewise doomed are

the tyrants of today who hold the human soul in terror and dismay. All this the prophets preached, and he who would proclaim the acceptable word of the Lord will first ground himself in the word of the prophets, as his Master before him did.

the Word ... OF THE SCHOLARS

I

In the House of ben Ezra

It was an impressive group that gathered in the house of the learned Aben ben Ezra that morning. Their faces identified them as men of sensitive spirits; their dress marked them as men of affairs; their dignified demeanor indicated that they were leaders. Above all, their conversation stamped them as intellectuals.

Yet they were slaves!

Something more than a century and a half before, their fathers, in a succession of incredibly stupid political maneuvers, had invited the awful wrath of Nebuchadrezzar, king of Babylonia; and under the hammer blows of one brief and terrible assault the beautiful capital Jerusalem was reduced to rubble, and thousands of the best citizens of Judah were deported to the valleys of the Tigris and Euphrates.

Not that they were brutally treated as deportees, for Babylonia accorded them surprisingly generous treatment, at least when measured by the standards of that day. They were allowed to live in their own communities, speak their own language, maintain their own culture, and foster their own institutions as long as they did not disturb the peace of the realm. Many took advantage of their opportunities and prospered.

They were never allowed to forget, however, that they were members of a subjugated race—just another nation under the heel of the conqueror. But for this Babylonia was not entirely to blame. There was something about the religion of the deportees which made them insoluble. Their racial pride survived all indignities, and though life alongside the brimming canals and amid the lush fields of the Tigris and Euphrates valleys offered advantages the narrow valleys and limestone hills of Judah could not provide, the deportees never ceased to sigh for their homeland. "How shall we sing the Lord's song in a strange land?" [25] they sobbed, and the rich livings of Babylonia were poor consolation for the loss of liberties. The Babylonians were never quite able to understand these strange people to whom, because they had come from the land of Judah, had been given the name "Jews." It has always been hard for a man with no convictions to understand another man who holds even a few.

The secret of the Jews' aloofness lay in a religious doctrine, profoundly believed, which declared that they had been vowed in perpetual loyalty to Jehovah, their God, by a Covenant sealed in the wilderness hundreds of years before by their nomadic great-grandsires. This conviction was the core of their intense nationalism; it set them apart forever from all men.

Three things they most steadfastly believed—that all the world, but particularly the Jews, lived under the authority of a moral order to which even kings, emperors, and empires were subject; that they had been created in the image of God and born with the mint mark of divinity upon them; that every Jew, as a Jew, was born to enjoy certain rights and privileges which endowed him with sanctity as an individual. Any people believing such majestic doctrines can never be permanently enslaved, and in the case of the Jews, as in the case of other subject races since, *their religion saved them*.

The little group of sober men which gathered that morning at the house of Aben ben Ezra were the religious leaders of the Jews—scribes, priests, prophets. With the doors of political privilege closed tight against them, with economic opportunities strictly circumscribed, and with the Covenant walling them in, it was inevitable that leadership among them would turn to religion as a means of self-expression, and ben Ezra's guests represented the most profound religious learning and the finest scholarship of the exiles.

Within a few short weeks following their arrival in Babylonia the deportees faced a spiritual problem of the first magnitude. According to the teachings of their ancient prophets and the terms of the Covenant sealed in the wilderness, the Hebrews were the chosen of God, assured of divine assistance, and destined to execute the will of Jehovah on earth. One of their most brilliant preachers, Isaiah, had even promised that Jerusalem would stand eternally in testimony to the power of God and the inviolability of the Covenant.[26] But there could be no blinking at the facts. Their nation was destroyed, their capital was in ruins, and they were slaves. What, then, was the explanation?

There could be but two possible solutions of the problem. They might conclude that Jehovah, their God, had not been equal to the emergency and had been compelled to bow before the superior might of Babylonian arms and Babylonian gods. This they steadfastly refused to believe. Or they might conclude that the nation's sins had alienated the favor of Jehovah, and that they had been deserted to their fate by an outraged God. This they accepted as the meaning of their misfortunes; and immediately historians, theologians, prophets, priests, and thinkers among them tackled the problem, with an earnestness seldom witnessed and never surpassed among men, in an effort to discover, if possible, wherein they had sinned. In the course of many years the scholars became a professional class, and later were called scribes.

It was not enough, however, to teach the people that they had sinned and merited the wrath of Jehovah. It was necessary now that they be instructed on the subject of *how* they had sinned if they were to live blamelessly in the future and earn redemption and restoration. This, then, also became the responsibility of the scribes, and Aben ben Ezra's guests had assembled that day to take counsel together on the subject, just as they had on so many occasions in the past.

II

The Meeting of the Elders

In recent years a crisis had been developing in the life of the people. Paganism had been crowding in upon them, seducing their children. Their sons were marrying comely Babylonian girls; prosperity was beginning to soften the shell of their racial exclusiveness; the consciousness of the Covenant was dimming. *They were ceasing to be Jews.*

Perhaps even more serious than the symptoms just mentioned was the fact that they were losing the sense of their national destiny. Jeremiah, the prophet of the last days, had promised that they would be returned to the Land of Promise eventually,[27] and a start of sorts had been made but with

45

little success. The barren, tawny hills of Judah yielded a living grudgingly, and the task of rebuilding the ruins of Jerusalem was a staggering one. Their fathers had sung: "If I forget thee, O Jerusalem, let my right hand forget her cunning. If I do not remember thee, let my tongue cleave to the roof of my mouth; if I prefer not Jerusalem above my chief joy." [28] Prophets, here and there, had preached eloquently to the people on the subject of the nation's destiny, and deep emotions had stirred within them for a time; but now they were fast lowering their national and religious consciousness, and the responsibility for devising some challenge by which the Jews could be called back to their sacred relationships rested squarely upon the shoulders of the religious leaders.

Such were Aben ben Ezra's guests, and such was the problem they faced that morning in the meeting of the elders.

According to the accepted rule of the ancient East, the heads of families composed the councils of the nations, but the leaders of the Jews who gathered that morning in the house of ben Ezra were men who had come to power and influence because of their reputation for wisdom and their devotion to the cause of Jehovah. Theirs was an intellectual and spiritual aristocracy, unlike anything to be found anywhere else in the world of that day. With all other doors closed to them, the great minds among the exiles had turned to religion, and to the rich historical and prophetic literature which had been saved from the wreckage of the kingdoms. The elders who assembled in ben Ezra's upper room were steeped in the promises of Isaiah, Jeremiah, and Hosea; they had pondered through long years on the majestic faith of Habakkuk; the hardships of servitude had interpreted for them the vivid social protests of Amos and Micah.

There is a sense in which they might have been called the conservatives of their day, but there are generations when conservatism is synonymous with salvation. The people must be called back to their ancient faith. The gathering that morning was a matter of supreme importance in the life of the Jews— as all their other meetings had been, for that matter. A nation's existence was at stake; the future of civilization was hanging in the balances. Try to imagine what it would have meant to us if they had not held those meetings, and if the faith of the Jews in a God of truth and justice had perished from among men, being absorbed into the paganism of Babylonia. The elders of the Jews could not possibly have foreseen all the meaning of their meeting, but at least they saw one necessity crystal clear: *The faith of Israel must be purified and preserved.*

The Jews had already worked one miracle in religious history. They had saved Jehovah from oblivion. Never before had the god of a defeated nation survived the destruction of the state. Exile had always been fatal to conquered divinities. But with the deportees who trekked across that awful way from Jerusalem to Babylon in 586 B.C., the last pitiful remnants of the once proud little state, there went the Spirit of the living God; and behold, when they settled down beside the "waters of Babylon," he was with them, *another exile!* Never before had a living divinity been carried across the borders into the land of a conquering nation, there to share the bondage of the defeated. But it happened among the Hebrews!

And now in the year 450 B.C. it had become the duty of the elders of Israel to call the nation back to the ancient hope —the Covenant, the kingdom, and the ancient destiny of the

Hebrews. A new beginning was to be made someday in the covenanted homeland. This meant that the blood stream of the Jews must be kept clean and uncontaminated by any admixture of pagan strains. Jehovah must have an untainted people with whom to work. This meant that intermarriage with the pagans must stop,[29] and that a worship pleasing to a God of holiness must be devised.

III

The Parchments

As the elders of Israel filed into the spacious upper room of ben Ezra's house to begin their discussions, a lad of some fourteen summers appeared through a door at the rear carrying about half a dozen rolls of parchment, each one carefully wrapped in a linen cloth. These he deposited upon a table and, turning, left the room. A few minutes later he appeared again, this time with more rolls, large and small, which he laid beside the first, handling them with the utmost care. A third armful deposited upon the great table brought the number to something more than a score. As his guests began settling themselves about the room, Aben ben Ezra proceeded to unwrap the rolls with something of the reverence that a saint might bestow upon the symbols of his faith.

For all the simplicity of their appearance, the evidences of age and much handling, those rolls represented drama, sacrifice, sentiment, and patriotism of the highest order, and there can be no adequate explanation of the amazing history of the Jews which omits the story. Indeed, there is no Christian in all the world today who is not indebted, beyond all his power to pay, to those devoted souls who preserved those rolls for the generations that have followed.

As the tragic survivors of the sacking of Jerusalem were being rounded up in the valley below the city that dreadful day in 586 B.C., preparatory to setting off on an awful trek across the desert to Babylonia, the uppermost question in the mind of every person was, "How much can I carry?" A generation that has seen Chinese, French, and Polish refugees streaming along country roads, with all their remaining possessions in bundles on their backs, may be able to picture in imagination some of the throbbing tragedy that was enacted in the little valley below Jerusalem as priceless and precious things were discarded in order to bring those packs down to bearable dimensions.

Something of the reverence with which the parchment rolls upon ben Ezra's table were handled by the elders of Israel may be sensed when it is known that they had been carried across the scorching, blinding, pitiless desert on the backs of their great-grandsires. Cloaks that promised some protection against the bitter cold of the desert nights had been left behind because there was neither room nor strength for carrying them *and* the rolls; in that hour of high decision, when a Babylonian spear was prodding them to be on their way, comfort was discarded in favor of faith, and the rolls were given the place cloaks might have had.

"Man shall not live by bread alone," the carpenter's son quoted, in the midst of a period of temptation in the wilderness when he was deciding the issue of his own life, and it is not impossible to believe that at that moment he was thinking of those unnamed heroes of Israel who chose rolls of parchment, whereon were written the great words of faith, in preference to cloaks that might have warmed their bodies, and in that choice saved for all generations to come the basic

49

documents of Jewish and Christian scriptures. Surely the God of truth guided those humble Hebrews that day in the valley below Jerusalem.

Thus it came about that when the prophets, priests, scribes, and elders of Israel sought an answer to their problem, How can the nation regain the favor of Jehovah? the great words of the Hebrew seers and sages of all the past were at hand to assist them.

There, upon the table before ben Ezra's guests, lay a copy of the Book of the Law which had been found in the temple during the reign of the good King Josiah.[30] Frayed and worn from much handling, it was the most treasured possession of the group. The precise circumstances under which the original volume had come into existence constituted a great mystery; but as the elders of Israel pored over the majestic lines inscribed upon the roll before them, they were moved to awe by the belief that they were reading words directly from Moses, the immortal leader of the Exodus.

It had been during those dark years of Manasseh,[31] the unspeakable, that members of the prophetic party had undertaken the writing. Harried by day and spied upon by night, their lives in daily danger,[32] they had contrived to meet from time to time in a secret rendezvous, there to pray for the salvation of Israel and plan for the nation's resurrection. Believing that a day would come when the bloody yoke would be lifted from their necks, they had spent long hours studying the ancient laws of Moses and adapting them to the needs they knew would exist when the nation had been delivered from the tyrant. Social in its outlook, loyal to the mind of Moses, prophetic in its form, and invested with the strange sanctity that comes with mystery, it was of incalculable value to the elders of the Exile, and around it they organized all their labors.

Then there were ancient histories of the nation which had been compiled by great thinkers of Israel and Judah, moving descriptions of the providence with which Jehovah had prepared the nation for its destiny and guided it through harrowing days. Some said Moses had had some hand in preparing them, and certainly they reflected his viewpoint; but regardless of their authorship, they were profoundly influential in shaping the great book upon which the elders were laboring.

Conspicuous in the pile was one great roll containing the sermons of Isaiah. What rare fortune that it had been saved! One old scribe's lips moved in a whispered prayer of thanksgiving that this roll had found a place upon the burdened back of one of the fathers in Israel more than a hundred years before. And there were lesser rolls whereon were written the flaming sentences of Amos and Micah, to say nothing of the huge roll containing the words of Jeremiah, the last of the great prophets of Judah. One of those smaller rolls had been written by Zephaniah when the frightful depredations of the Scythians made it appear that all the earth was to be scorched and nothing left alive. And there was Nahum's roll commemorating the fall of Nineveh.

True, there were among the rolls upon the table a few which had been written by great souls who had suffered and meditated in the midst of the Exile. Ezekiel, the priest, was represented by a roll containing an exalted code which he proposed should govern the restored nation.[33] Then there was the roll from the hand of an unnamed prophet of the Exile who had composed a sublime hymn about the suffering of a "servant" of Jehovah.[34] Temple annals, royal records, sermons, psalms, histories, legal codes—they were all there for the inspiration and guidance of the elders of Israel upon whom there rested the responsibility for rehabilitating the faith and furnishing the leadership of the disintegrating nation.

As the learned elders gathered in ben Ezra's upper room to plan the nation's future, the record of its past was before them. The story of the Lord's dealings with his people was written upon those parchments that wise men might read and understand.

IV

In Search of an Answer

They were no starry-eyed dreamers or ecstatic dervishes who gathered in that upper room that morning. Their faces were toward the light, and their souls were afire, but their feet were upon the ground. They knew a mirage when they saw it.

First of all, they were well aware of the fact that they were confronted by a world state so powerful that no man dared defy its might. To dream of re-establishing the little kingdom of Judah, under those circumstances and under the very eyes of the empire, called for statesmanship and skill of rare quality. Ruthlessness and naked force had to be circumvented; their masters must be made their allies.

Above all, they were men of magnificent faith; but this, in turn, was the product of their scholarship. No man is so strong or so capable as *the man who knows*; and the long hours and patient years they had spent, quarrying among the rolls of history, law, and prophecy, had convinced them that the nation's great day of destiny was still in the future. They might live in a small corner of the world, but they had distilled the experience of the centuries for their wisdom. To a politician the nation's plight was hopeless, and to an economist it was altogether without a solution, but to devout and pious men whose minds had been illuminated by a faith based on knowledge, no wrong was eternal; and *the elders of Israel dared to believe.*

This is not to say, of course, that they were blind optimists who had stared at the sun until all their tears had been licked away. Rather, they were heroic souls who had faced the bitter facts of the Exile as Jacob faced his adversary, saying, "I will not let thee go, except thou bless me." [35] The problem they faced has staggered the best minds of all generations—Why do good men suffer?

In the case of the Jews, however, the issue assumed a particular form: Has the Covenant been suspended? Is our God powerless to prevent the disaster that has overtaken us? Has the nation been abandoned to its fate?

These were not questions to be answered on the basis of easy emotionalism or cheap sentimentality. Instead, they were problems that called for the most serious thought of which a devout and honest mind is capable. They dared not ignore one fact! Not one bit of logic could be evaded! Every reason must be tested! Questions such as these called for the most courageous minds.

Having made their faith in the character of God secure, their next problem was almost equally complicated: If the nation has alienated the favor of Yahweh through sin, how can it restore itself to his favor?

We cannot explore in detail the solution of the problem which was finally offered by the elders of Israel. Rather, our interest in the case is confined to the fact that *the solution was worked out by scholars.* It was an accomplishment in which plain men had tremendous stakes, but it was one in which they could not share. Their security, however, was based on the fact that the solution had been worked out by learned men who faced all the facts and recognized all the questions involved. And this, indeed, is the position of plain men of faith in every generation.

The major convictions of religion derive their stability from whatever support they may have from the thinkers. And at this point the Christian preacher may take heart. Those who worship a God of truth make room in their theology for everything true. Most of us, perhaps, find some difficulty in following the philosophers and metaphysicians in all their technical terminology and the ramifications of their logic. But of one thing we may rest assured: Christian thinkers have gone as far out into the realms of philosophical speculation and theory as any human minds have gone, and *they have come back with their faith unshaken.* It is reassuring to hear them say, "There is nothing out there to fear." The unknown holds no terrors for them. In some few particulars—for instance, in the case of immortality—they frankly say, "We cannot prove it"; but immediately they hasten to add, "Nor can atheism disprove it." All this means that plain men of Christian faith can face the skeptics unafraid and say, "Ask the scholars; they have the answers!"

The sages who gathered in ben Ezra's upper room in Babylon that fateful morning, more than four hundred years before Christ, were not the rabble rousers of their day. Neither were they the inciters of mobs. Instead, they were the most stable and best-trained minds among the Jews. They knew their books, the sacred rolls that had come out of Judah on the backs of their great-grandsires. Moreover, they had at least a general knowledge and understanding of the best philosophic thought of the Babylonians, and they had measured their Yahwistic concepts alongside the finest that paganism could offer. If, in the great Book of the Law which they finally gave to the nation, there are occasional evidences of borrowing from Babylonian sources, this need not occasion any surprise nor raise any fears. If they were within their rights in using Babylonian parchment upon which to record their convictions, they were also justified in using Babylonian literary devices to express their ideas, if any such could be made to serve the cause of truth.

It is somewhere about this time in the history of God's people that the man who would "preach the word" picks up the trail of the scholars. The careful reader of the Old Testament must have been deeply impressed with the story found in Nehemiah of the proclamation of the Book of the Law as the constitution of the Jews.[36] Thereafter they became "the people of the book." Its laws, concepts, and ideals were the rock base of all their subsequent culture and conviction. Israel was a nation *saved by a book, and that book was the work of the scholars!* Elders such as those who gathered in Aben ben Ezra's upper room became the saviors of their people and, in time, the progenitors of our Christian faith. Our destiny rested with them.

v

The Book of the Law

If any man is interested in taking the mental measure of those ancient elders of Israel, let him make a careful study of the Book of the Law which they handed down to us. It is extant and current among us, being contained in the first five books of the Old Testament, often called the Pentateuch.

To determine delicate and complicated questions of Pentateuchal authorship is not our aim here. It is sufficient for our purpose to know that great scholars of the Exile, drawing upon all the literary and religious treasures of the nation, and making use of histories, prophecies, legal codes, and declarations of faith, compiled the Book of the Law, and that it was accepted by the Jews, in a spectacular ceremony of the utmost solemnity, as their constitution, scripture, civil code, and basis of life.

There is, after all, only a small difference between the one who first conceives a great idea and the one who appreciates it afterward. One of Israel's great poets once said that "deep calleth unto deep," and he might have added that the deep also calls to the shallow, but the shallow do not hear because they are shallow. At least something of the majestic sweep of the minds of those ancient scholars may be sensed by considering the profound import of that which they saved out of the mass of literature before them.

There is an impressive revelation of the vastness of their minds in those ten massive words with which the Book of the Law opens: *"In the beginning God created the heaven and the earth."*

The mind that first framed this utterance, and the minds that later saved it from oblivion by incorporating it into the Book of the Law, could have been but "little lower than the angels." With all the accumulated learning of the centuries, and with all the thinking of the greatest minds of the race at our disposal, we discover that the horizon of knowledge has never been pushed farther back than by that solemn declaration. And whether that momentous judgment was first expressed by Moses or by some other man under the guidance of God, the greatness of the minds of Israel's elders is revealed in the fact that they apprehended the eternal significance of those ten words and set them at the head of their book.

History is an inspiring teacher of faith, and we can well afford at this point to pause for just a moment and look back over the long and tortuous course by which our scriptures containing "the word" have come down to us. It is probable that, had there been a commentator to report the tragedy of Jerusalem in 586 B.C., he would have announced the end of the little kingdom of Judah. To all appearances the curtain had rung down upon a "noble experiment." Babylonia ruled the world, and the children of Abraham had been swallowed up in disaster, never to be heard from again. But contemporary judgments are seldom safe, and the nation that builds its faith on this morning's headlines is headed for disaster, for there are always new headlines tomorrow morning.

Where are the Babylonians today, or the Assyrians, or the Syrians, or the Egyptians, or any of the ancient mighty ones who led Israel and Judah "like lambs to the slaughter"? Gone is Nineveh, Thebes, Babylon, Tyre! But the Jews we have with us everywhere—a nation saved by a book!

So we pause at the first milepost to pay our tribute to those devoted scholars of the Exile who produced the Book of the Law, compiling it from the accumulated literary treasures and spiritual experiences of a race that has from the beginning relied for its existence upon its genius for religion.

VI

Transplanting a Great Faith

In the year 356 B.C. a son was born in the home of Philip, king of Macedonia, to whom was given the name Alexander. At the age of sixteen he was left in charge of the government while his father marched against Byzantium, and thus at an early age he tasted the intoxicant of power. Four years later, upon the assassination of Philip, he ascended to the throne as the king of the Hellenic world, and immediately launched out upon a career so spectacular that history ever since has accorded him the title "The Great."

His empire was broken up soon after his death, but in the meantime he had founded Greek cities and colonies everywhere. The Greek language, because of his enthusiasm for the spread of Greek culture, had become the speech of government and literature throughout the entire East, which was, in many respects, the world. It was a period of ferment, with populations moving or being moved, and cities rising and falling. Because of their geographical location astride the southern tip of the Fertile Crescent, it was impossible for the Jews to hold aloof from world affairs, and the Greek period saw Jewish colonies founded in far places.

In the year 332 B.C. Alexander planned the city of Alexandria, in Egypt; and in appreciation of certain assistance which had been given him he ordered that all Jewish citizens of the new metropolis should be granted certain exemptions from taxation and be accorded many other coveted special privileges. He even went to great pains to build up a powerful colony of them within the city, so that it became one of the great Jewish centers of the world, taking rank alongside Jerusalem itself. In particular, the Hebrew university of Alexandria became world famous as a seat of learning.

With Jews dispersed throughout the world, their children growing up to speak alien tongues, the day came when the sacred scriptures written in Hebrew were a sealed book to millions. Only a fraction of the race throughout the world was able to read them in the original language. On great holy occasions, when pilgrims returned to Jerusalem from the ends of the earth to observe the Feast of the Passover or other festal days, the number of those who could converse in Hebrew or read the literature of the nation in the mother tongue was a relatively small fraction of the multitude assembled. The hand of death was already upon the Hebrew language. Any thoughtful man could see that something had to be done.

Something was done. Just how it was done is shrouded in much uncertainty, and the exact facts probably will never be known. In the absence of any historical records in the case we must be content with many surmises. But of one great fact we can be absolutely sure: *The Hebrew scriptures, which now included much beside the Book of the Law, were translated into Greek and were put within the reach of the common people everywhere.*

The modern preacher is apt to pass over this truly remarkable achievement, giving it little more than a passing thought. But no man who undertakes to "preach the word" can afford to ignore two monumental facts associated therewith.

In the first place we have, in the translation of the Hebrew scriptures from the tongue in which they were written into the Greek of the everyday speech, the transplanting of a religious faith on a scale perhaps unprecedented. Here was a cross-fertilization of the spiritual life of the world such as had never before been attempted. True, the Jews had learned much from Babylonia, but that had been learned in the Babylonian speech. In this case Hebrew ideas were moved out of their mother tongue into an alien speech and made indigenous in a Greek world and available to all men of all races. The ancient protests of the eighth-century prophets, the Holiness Code worked out by the subjugated in Babylonia, the rich devotional literature of the Psalms, which represented the spiritual aspirations of the people through many centuries, the prophetic teachings of Joshua, Judges, and the great Book of the Kings (I and II Samuel, I and II Kings), were all carried over into the idioms and thought forms of the Greek language.

The modern Christian, accustomed as he is to the justifiable pride with which the American Bible Society announces that the Scriptures are now available in more than a thousand languages, finds it difficult to appreciate the full significance of that first translation. Today we move as easily from one language to another as we do from one state to another, but in the third century before Christ the emancipation of the Jewish scriptures from the limitations of the Hebrew language was high adventure!

The second fact of which we need to be reminded is that the task of translating the sacred writings was *assigned to the scholars*. The student of biblical criticism may be excused for lamenting, perhaps rather loudly, our almost complete lack of exact information relative to most details. Who ordered the translation? Who chose the translators? When was it done? Where was it done? How much time did the task require? To none of these questions can we give any exact answer. An old legend has it that seventy scholars completed the work in seventy days, and to this bit of fancy we owe the name by which the finished version is generally known—the Septuagint—but careful students long ago abandoned all confidence in the legend because there are no credible facts to support it.

The Septuagint is, however, its own best credential. Modern scholars skilled in Hebrew and Greek are agreed that a translation so excellent and so satisfactory could not have been produced by any but the most learned. Whoever those ancient worthies may have been we cannot tell, but at least this we know—they were masters of their craft. With the utmost reverence and respect they lifted the Book of the Law, the writings of the prophets, and ancient devotional psalms of the people, out of their native Hebrew and transplanted them into the warm, hospitable soil of the plain man's speech—Greek.

Again we pause to pay our humble tribute to the scholars. They conveyed to us writings which contain the word we are to preach, and in doing so they exercised a liberalism of mind comparable only to that of the great prophets themselves.

VII

The First Christian Translation

It was inevitable that those first-century Christians, having been reared upon and nourished by the Hebrew scriptures, should in turn produce their own sacred writings. By the time the Christian movement had rounded out its first century of existence, Christian thinkers had produced the bulk, if not the entirety, of our New Testament.

There is some danger that the modern Christian may make the mistake of assuming that the New Testament produced the Christian Church, whereas the fact is, of course, that the

Christian Church produced the New Testament; and in that connection we find another item in our indebtedness to scholars, for the New Testament was written by such.

The first piece of Christian writing to come into existence, according to the best information now available to us, was one of Paul's letters. Whether it was First Thessalonians or the Epistle to the Galatians is in doubt, but in either case it was the product of one of the finest minds the race has ever produced. Born in Tarsus, schooled in Jerusalem by that great master of the Law, Gamaliel,[37] familiar with Greek learning and philosophy, saturated with the sacred lore of the Jews, a Roman citizen with all roads open unto him, the Apostle Paul takes rank with the greatest minds of the ages. None but the ignorant or prejudiced would deny to him the title of scholar.

Then there is that magnificent mind back of the Fourth Gospel. The question of his precise identity is unsettled, but there is no question of the fact that in John's Gospel we are face to face with one of the most profound pieces of writing ever to be committed to manuscript by a human hand. There is something of the quality of Genesis about the writer, as he opens his treatise with the solemn declaration, "In the beginning was the Word." A more extended investigation of his testimony must be reserved until our next chapter, but at least one thing can be said at this point—the world will never be able to escape the moral and spiritual implications of that monumental statement he makes in his first chapter: *The Word became flesh, and dwelt among us.*[38] If there is any question as to the dimensions of the writer's mind, let us be reminded that the greatest intellects of eighteen centuries have been quarrying doctrines from his Gospel and have not yet exhausted it. Indeed, it is only now coming into its own.

Time and space do not permit us to pay tribute to all those rich and rare minds to whom we are indebted for our New Testament. Luke, the historian; another John, the revealer; Matthew, the interpreter of the Messiah; and the unknown author of Hebrews—to these and others whose testimonies have been incorporated into Holy Writ we offer our humble tribute of admiration and respect. There is not a commonplace soul or intellect among them.

There came a day, however, when the Christian scriptures had to undergo the same transplanting the Hebrew writings had experienced. It became necessary to translate them.

The Greek world of Alexander the Great was passing. Roman roads, Roman legions, Roman commerce, and Roman civil government had taken possession of the world and altered the manner of living for all men everywhere. The seat of authority for the Christian Church had moved from east to west and was finally established in Rome. The bishop of the church at the capital was in process of becoming the pope of the Christian Church of all the world. It was inevitable that the New Testament would have to be translated out of its native Greek into the Latin of the common people, and once more religion turned to the scholars for assistance and guidance.

There was, toward the close of the fourth century of the Christian era, one individual who towered above the rest of the race in scholarship, as a mountain towers above the plain. History knows him as St. Jerome, but his contemporaries knew him as the greatest scholar of the age. To this master of Hebrew, Greek, Latin, philosophy, rhetoric, and theology was delegated the delicate and highly responsible task of transferring the ancient religious writings of the Jews and the more modern scriptures of the Christians from the Hebrew and the Greek over into the vernacular of the common people.

As early as A.D. 385 that great saint and scholar had become deeply interested in the project and had done much preliminary work in the field; but when the church officially commissioned him to direct the task, he immediately gathered about him a company of the best-trained scholars of his day, and together they set about the matter. Anyone interested in the details of the story should read the complete record in some good church history. It is sufficient for our purpose to know that the little band of savants under Jerome's direction represented the most profound learning the fifth-century Christian world could muster. Again it must be said that they were not the rabble rousers, the cultists, the advertisers, or the self-appointed dictators of doctrine. Rather they were the cultured product of the finest universities, the most matured thinkers in the Christian world, the most scientific-minded of their generation.

And the humble and the poor were their beneficiaries!

It is highly significant that the version of the Hebrew Old Testament and the Greek New Testament which they produced should have come to be known as the "Vulgate"—the scriptures of the vulgar (common) people. And from that day to this, when unlettered and unschooled men have gathered their little ones about them in such scenes as that portrayed by Robert Burns in "The Cotter's Saturday Night," somewhere in the shadows the scholars have stood and smiled. It has been their labors that have put the Holy Scriptures within the reach and understanding of humble men when they teach their children the way of life.

VIII

The King James Version

In the year 1611 English Protestantism witnessed the climax of a long-protracted effort on the part of the scholars to transfer the Holy Scriptures once again from one language to another. This time it was to be from the stately Latin into the conventional English of the seventeenth century.

Early efforts in this direction had encountered many difficulties, in the process of which some of the choicest spirits of the English-speaking world had earned entry into the ranks of the martyrs. Wycliffe, Tyndale, Miles Coverdale—to name but three—paid with "blood, toil, tears, and sweat" for their temerity in attempting to put the Bible into the speech of the plain people without the authority of the English church. But the tide could not be held back indefinitely; finally by the authority of King James, himself a scholar of parts, the enterprise got under way, and in 1611 the Authorized Version was offered to the English public by royal decree.

To all those who decry modern translations of the Holy Scriptures, preferring the Authorized Version, at least this much should be said: *The King James Version of the Holy Bible was the product of the finest English scholarship of the early seventeenth century*. He who would honor those translators for their faithful and immortal work will avail himself of the findings of modern scholars who have built upon the foundations they laid.

We cannot here go into the conditions that have arisen to warrant the recent undertaking of a new and revised American translation of the Holy Bible. The reasons have been pretty thoroughly explained by highly qualified writers. It remains to add but one final word in paying tribute to the long list of great names to whom we are indebted for our Scriptures.

No book in all the world has been subjected to such searching scrutiny as the Bible. There is not a line, word, or even letter that has not been studied with infinite care. The book has come up the hard way; and as the humble Christian reads it in the evening time for consolation, comfort, or guidance, he may be confident that he is reading a text that has stood every test. We can more certainly be sure of the words of Jesus than we can of the words of Socrates or Plato.

You can trust your Bible! You have the word of the scholars for that! They know!

Preach the word! The word of the scholars!

the Word ... OF THE APOSTLES

I

A Christian Appears at Ephesus

One lovely day in the spring, it may have been about
A.D. 40, a stranger appeared in the market place of Ephesus
and, having gathered a little company of listeners about him,
told an amazing story. He said he was from the Jewish province of Galilee, just south of Syria, and that was against him
from the start, for Jews were none too popular anywhere in
the Roman Empire. The sophisticated Ephesians forgot their
prejudices for the moment, however, and listened to him with
profound interest because of the thrilling tale he told. All this
was according to the custom of Ephesus, and the stranger was
only one more in the long succession of street preachers who
had held forth in the crowded market place, expounding weird
doctrines and explaining mysterious ceremonies believed and
practiced in far places of the earth.

It was a time of great spiritual restlessness throughout the
world. The religions of the East had utterly failed, and the
souls of men were on the march, searching for some sure answer to the relentless questions that surge up in the minds of
men of every generation. The city of Ephesus stood at a cross-
roads, and the ideas of all the world contended in the market
place for the loyalties of thoughtful people. Thus it happened

that any preacher or teacher who had a faith to offer might be reasonably sure of an audience in Ephesus, if only for an hour.

The newcomer, however, seemed to be very different from the others who had harangued the crowds in the market place of Ephesus. In the first place, there was high fervor in his words which set him wide apart from the superficial dilettantes who taught trivialities for the entertainment and amusement of the multitudes. From beginning to end his speech was saturated with a spirit of desperation which was very compelling. He talked like a man possessed, as though his soul's salvation depended upon the delivery of his message, and the passion in his words completely captivated the crowd. Just here, perhaps, was a large part of the secret of his power—he seemed to believe that the thing he was saying *must be said.*

In the second place, he had no begging bowl. Ordinarily the street preachers to whom Ephesus was accustomed would climax their diatribes with a fervent appeal for alms and pass a little earthen bowl among the listeners in the hope of collecting a few small coins as payment for their ministry. Some of the more famous among them resorted to more refined devices; they hired halls and charged impressive fees, but their ultimate object was the same. Not so this preacher, who refused to accept any alms.[39] He was absorbed in his message.

At the close of his address a number of the more serious-minded of his listeners tarried to ask questions. It was very evident that his story had made a deep impression upon them, and they sought additional information with unfeigned eagerness. As the preacher answered their questions and dilated somewhat upon details, others joined the circle, and soon the stranger found himself under the necessity of telling his tale again in order to explain the subject of the conversation. Thus it went on—the story, questions, exposition, newcomers, more questions, and the story again.

II
The Story He Told

The recital that day in the market place of Ephesus had to do with an astounding occurrence in Palestine only a few years before:

A prophet appeared in the province of Galilee and attracted much attention with preaching which was unusually winsome and heartening. Although he had none of the formal training usually acquired by learned doctors of the Law, he spoke about the deep things of the spirit with an authority that could not be ignored, and the plain people flocked to hear him.

Various wonders followed his preaching. Men possessed by demons were freed from their tortures; the lame were healed and sent on their way well and strong again; sight was restored to the blind; ailments which had resisted the best efforts of the physicians surrendered to a single word, spoken with startling power.

The province of Galilee was itself an unusual section of Palestine. Removed as they were from the religious professionalism of Jerusalem and its temple, the people of the province had absorbed more of the prevailing Greek culture than their Judean neighbors. Intoxicating ideas of liberty and freedom fermented in their minds, and fascinating speculations concerning life and the spiritual world stimulated a certain intellectual independence which expressed itself in a variety of ways. On more than one occasion Caesar had been under the necessity of dispatching reinforcements to Galilee to put down uprisings of radicals of one kind and another. To be a

Galilean was to be under suspicion both in Jerusalem and in Rome. The prophet, however, was concerned with none of this, though at least one radical (Simon the Zealot [40]) was a member of the little group of devoted friends who joined him and traveled about the countryside with him. Instead, he occupied himself with preaching and teaching the multitudes about a new way of life which he called "the kingdom of heaven."

It was not alone that he worked miracles but, far more important, that he had raised a great hope among the plain people. There were those who believed he was the promised Messiah of the Jews who was to restore the nation to power and, perhaps, even supplant Rome. When they were pressed in the matter, they had to admit that he did few of the things the Messiah was expected to do, for he raised no armies, headed no revolutionary movement, and made no political promises. Instead, he talked about the ways by which a man might find God, how one might live in peace with his fellows, and what attitudes one should take toward money, one's enemies, and the underdogs of the world. All this had the effect of raising a great longing within the hearts of the people for a better world—one in which the will of God would be done among men—and there were those who solemnly believed he was about to set up such a new order. Everywhere he preached there was a rising resentment against wrong; his hearers were always left with a wistful longing after righteousness and an impatience with evil.

As was to be expected, there was a wide variety of opinion concerning him among those who heard him. Some said he was one of the prophets come back to life again,[41] others that he was one of the princes of evil bent on destroying the ancient faith and leading the people astray.[42] A few seemed to sense a certain connection which they could not quite define between him and the Divine. But all, even his enemies, agreed that he was no ordinary man.

In the course of his career as a wandering preacher he incurred the enmity of the authorities. The civil government feared his popularity with the masses, and the religious leaders resented the superior attitude he assumed toward the Law and the temple. His doctrines, they feared, might undermine the religious traditions of Israel. The priests became anxious lest he jeopardize their privileged position; the doctors of the Law instinctively felt his contempt for their superficialities; the temple hierarchy were quick to sense the threat to their revenues implied in his preaching; and the respectable resented his including the underdogs in his scheme of salvation.

What he actually attempted to do was to invest piety with a new meaning. Moses had commanded, "Thou shalt not commit adultery," but the prophet of Galilee said that not only was the lustful act sinful but also equally sinful was the evil desire which lacked only an opportunity for gratification.[43] Covetousness he put on a par with stealing, and hate was equivalent to murder. At the same time he opened the door wide for sinners and outcasts and assured them that God's heart could always be touched by their penitence. In other words, the inner desire and not the outward act was the credential which a man might offer to God in token of his loyalty.

All this was, of course, revolutionary in a day when the highest religious authorities among the Jews taught that purity was a matter of physical cleanliness and that piety consisted

71

of a perfect performance of an infinite variety of ceremonial laws. And as the spiritual leaders among the Jews saw the masses rushing off after this unschooled and unauthorized prophet from Nazareth—the son of a carpenter—their fury and their fear knew no bounds. As usually happens in such a case, they identified their own special privileges with the stability of the Almighty, and in protecting their own position they thought they were coming to the defense of the Most High.

The story was too long to tell in detail, and in fact the stranger in the Ephesian market place told little more than the principal facts that first day.

At any rate, the rulers of the Jews managed by devious ways to contrive the death of the prophet. By suborning witnesses, by disguising their real motives, by threatening and intimidating, and by ignoring the actual evidence in the case, they managed to browbeat the Roman procurator into accepting their judgment so that he pronounced the death sentence. Even then it was because he thought he was saving the city from a riot that he gave his consent.

An unholy alliance manipulated the prophet's doom. In the course of a farcical trial the Roman and the Jewish law was breached at least twenty-two times. A capitalist whose personal fortune was threatened instigated the proceedings. A high priest whose appointment had been secured from Rome at the cost of a huge bribe lent legal sanction by finding a loophole in the law which could be twisted to justify the death sentence. A playboy king, accompanied by his wife by an incestuous marriage, dismissed the affair when he might have saved the prophet, because the prophet would not entertain with a miracle.[44] A cringing politician, frightened at the pros-

72

pect of a riot if he did not meet the crowd's demands, passed the sentence that nailed the prophet to a cross, and then tried to disclaim all responsibility for the crime.

Up to this point the story the stranger told was interesting, of course, but it was not one to set Ephesus agog. The times were well acquainted with brutality and injustice. The ancient East had listened to other teachers, some of whom had incurred the suspicion of the authorities. Indeed, not a few had aroused the wrath of the empire for one reason or another and had died upon crosses charged with the crime of having incited insurrection, though it was not often that Rome accommodated the jealousy of local leaders to such an extent that the death sentence was passed to please them. After all, it might be better that one should die than that an unseemly riot should bring great Caesar's wrath down upon an entire province. In the case of the Galilean prophet, however, the greatest miracle of his life had occurred after his death.

III

The Amazing Story of the Resurrection

The stranger told his story with the skill of a great artist. It was very evident that he had told it many times before, and in the process of retelling, it had become a classic in reporting.

As the sun settled into the west, with less than an hour of light left on the eve of the Sabbath, it was discovered that the prophet was dead. The Roman guards, well accustomed to watching men die, had broken the leg bones of two thieves who hung from near-by crosses in order to hurry their death, but when they came to the cross upon which the prophet hung they discovered him dead already. It was necessary only to take his inert body down from the cross, and this some friends did, having received permission from the procurator. Then in hurried fashion they prepared it for burial, laid it hastily in a new tomb borrowed from an admirer, and afterward hastened back to the city to keep the Sabbath.

Through a night and a day and a night they remained in hiding, knowing full well that it was not safe in Jerusalem to be known as friends of one who had been crucified on the charge of having incited insurrection. On the second morning following the burial, however, some of their number made an early trip to his tomb and *found it empty*. Not long afterward a woman, and still later some men, *saw him alive!*

This was the part of the stranger's story which arrested the attention of the sophisticated Ephesians. Indeed, it was capturing the attention of men all over the East, for there was scarcely a city or village in the entire empire in which the tale was not being told. *A man who had died upon a cross, whose side had been pierced with a spear so that blood and water gushed forth—a sure proof of death—was alive again!*

If the evidence in the case rested on the testimony of two or three friends, this astonishing tale might be dismissed as a conspiracy to keep his memory alive, an invention by which the tellers thereof might hope to profit in some way. But hundreds saw him! At one time he appeared to a company of almost five hundred persons,[45] each one of whom was willing to take an oath that it was true—*he was alive!* On several other occasions he was seen by groups, all members of which were agreed on the essential fact that they had seen him and they knew he was alive.

It would not be possible, even today, to ignore a man who had been dead and was alive again. The very fact of his resurrection would call up a whole catalogue of questions, and so it was in the market place of Ephesus that day. Again and again the stranger from Galilee was interrupted by questions. "Who was this man?" "What was he like?" "What did he teach?" "What was the source of his authority?" "What gave him his power?" "Was he one of the gods?" "What did the Jews think about him?" "Where is he now?" "Has anyone seen him lately?"

The travel-stained preacher in the market place of Ephesus was not the only one who was going about the world telling this amazing story. Indeed, at that very moment, in many other cities other preachers were standing up before crowds in the bazaars and market places, telling the story of the prophet of Galilee who had been raised from the dead and who was alive among men. From the Tigris and Euphrates valleys in the east to the muddy Tiber in the west the story of the resurrection of Jesus of Nazareth was stirring the world.

Among the prophet's followers it was commonly believed that he was the Messiah of the Jews, but that was hard to believe. In the first place, none of the prophets had ever hinted that the Messiah would come out of Nazareth. Moreover, it was difficult to reconcile the idea of a triumphant Messiah with one who had died like a felon on one of Rome's crosses. Of course it was true that numerous prophecies had had their fulfillment in him, but even when the last possible adaptation of the prophetic word had been made to justify the claim, there was still a long list of unanswered questions left to puzzle the minds of the thoughtful.

For that matter, however, Ephesus was little interested in a Jewish Messiah; for, aside from the small colony of Jews who lived alongside the market place, the Ephesians were mostly Greeks who had been reared in the traditions of Greek culture and philosophy and had scarcely heard of the hope which had sustained Israel through five hundred years. They had never prayed for deliverance through long hours of horror; they had never known bondage and exile; they had never fed their souls on the faith that God would establish the rule of Israel throughout the earth as preached by the prophets. The doctrine of "the anointed of God" aroused no glowing response in their hearts, for they had never known frustration and bitter defeat. This was all alien to them.

But the preacher from Galilee declared that the crucified prophet was more than a Jewish Messiah. Indeed, he insisted, *he was the Son of God*—Deity who had assumed the form of a man for a few brief years in order to reveal the divine will and purposes to humanity.

While it is true that the story of the resurrection moved the Ephesians profoundly, almost equally impressive was the preacher's testimony concerning his own spiritual experience. He had, he said, accepted the prophet as his master and, in doing so, had found a new life flowing in upon him. To men familiar with Greek philosophy this was of the deepest interest, for the Greek mind was ever fond of playing with the idea of life and its origins. No preacher ever had more rapt attention when addressing Greeks than when he was discussing the source of life and the meaning of living.

At this point the preacher spoke as a man will who is sure of his ground; he was talking of something of which he was confident. Others might theorize, *but he knew*. A new spirit had come in upon him, he asserted, and from that day forward he had lived with an entirely new sense of power. Gone was the old sense of sin, and in its place had come a confidence that at last he was living in harmony with the Divine. That word "harmony," like the word "life," found an eager reception among the Greeks, for it too was one which fascinated them because of its speculative possibilities. All in all, as the preacher discoursed upon the subject of the resurrection, the risen Jesus, the new life, and the new sense of power, it was evident that he was making an impression upon the Ephesians. He was talking to them on a subject concerning which they had thought deeply and wistfully for many years.

IV

Ephesus Was Interested

The city of Ephesus, standing as it did facing Greece, and being the great metropolis of the East with trade routes converging upon it from every direction, was not unused to street preaching. In fact, at one time or another, most of the great orators of the day had appeared in the city to discuss their favorite themes, great and small, for the entertainment of the public. Preachers from distant cities—north, east, south, and west—had been present in the famous Ephesian lecture halls, partly for the purpose of debating with the learned ones gathered there, and partly in the hope that they might win Ephesian approval and thereby enhance their reputations, for to be accepted in Ephesus was only slightly less an honor than to be accepted in Athens itself.

Nowhere else in the world, perhaps in any century, has the orator been as popular as he was among the Greeks of the first century of the Christian era. Many of those wandering lecturers and preachers who appeared on the rostrums of Ephesus to lecture to the elite were superb masters of their profession. Their perfectly modulated voices, their dramatic artistry, and a certain skill in what is called psychology by moderns, made them extremely effective. It is true, of course, that some were no better than charlatans of dubious morals, but others were genuinely learned men who delivered thoughtful messages in complete sincerity. Still others might be classed as students of world affairs, for they brought to their listeners news of politics, economics, trade, and military adventures in far places of the earth. That was the only way news got about in the ancient East.

One reason why the preacher from Galilee was accorded so interested a hearing in Ephesus was that the minds of the East were wide open to new doctrines. The religious faiths of Greeks, Romans, and Egyptians were far spent. The pagan gods which had once been the recipients of reverent worship were being burlesqued on the stages of the theaters, and rare indeed is the divinity that can outlive ridicule. The Roman Empire, with its highly mobile legions recruited from a dozen races, had brought order out of political chaos and had established a form of peace—the *pax Romana*—throughout the whole Mediterranean area. Men's lives and property were secure, but their souls were bound by a great fear. Spiritual security they did not know.

A religious awakening was in progress throughout the East, with various ethical movements attracting considerable numbers of thoughtful people. The ancient religions had so far lost their hold upon serious-minded folk that no one ever thought of turning to the professional priests or to the temples for spiritual guidance in personal problems. Instead, a profession of teachers of ethics had arisen, not entirely unlike modern psychological counselors, and these were seeking as best they knew to assist the people in mastering life. Everywhere there was an eagerness to establish some kind of contact with the Divine. Interest in the question of personal immortality was at high tide. Life for millions was uprooted by the political and economic changes which had turned the world upside down, and men of all classes and cultures were searching heaven and earth for spiritual security.

It was as if the ground had been divinely prepared for the preaching of the stranger in the Ephesian market place, and above all things else, *he was sure of his message*. Others might theorize, speculate, and say, "I think." This man, true to the Christian movement of which he was a part, said, *"I know."*

Especially noticeable was the fact that he did not argue about a new doctrine. *He proclaimed a new life,* stoutly asserting that it had come in upon him from the moment he had submitted to the mastery of the prophet of Galilee, and that it was available to any other soul who was willing to pay its cost and accept its implications.

Who was the preacher from Galilee? The answer is that he may have been any one of hundreds of them, for they were a considerable company. He was the herald of a new age in which a new way of life was to prevail, and in which men were to be ushered into a new order—the kingdom of heaven. They were of various occupations, but they all had one calling—to preach the word. They were missionaries of a new way of life. In Antioch of Syria they were called Christians because of the name of the prophet to whom they had vowed their life and loyalty, and whom they called Lord—Jesus Christ.[46] And since they were themselves content with that name and made it an honored designation, it will be sufficient for us to call the stranger merely a Christian, a preacher of the word, one of the early disciples who pioneered the faith and proclaimed it with confidence to the ears of a wondering and wistful world.

It should be said, moreover, that these Christian evangelists were altogether unorganized. No committee passed on the question of any man's right to bear the name of Jesus, or to preach by his commission. No official hands were laid upon them, authorizing them to proclaim the news. No council met to define their message, or to pass upon the accuracy of their interpretation of the Master. Each was, in a very large measure, a law unto himself, the judge of his own orthodoxy, the final arbiter of his own theology. There came a time, of course, when strict lines were drawn, and when those who set out to preach the word were examined with meticulous care; but in the beginning, about the time the stranger appeared in Ephesus announcing that the crucified prophet had risen from the dead, any man might speak in the name of Jesus of Nazareth, and no one had the right to bid him hold his peace.

There were even a few women among them—elect ladies of brilliant mind, compelling personality, and vivid evidences of rare spiritual graces. There was, for instance, Priscilla, the wife of Aquila the tentmaker, whose vigorous and forceful personality made itself felt far beyond the confines of her home city of Corinth. Then there was Lydia, the seller of dyes, whose talent for trade distinguished her in the commercial life of the East. And there were also the daughters of Philip of Caesarea, who because of their rich spiritual graces were rated as prophetesses among the Christians.[47]

At this distance in time it is a little difficult to form any adequate impression of the bitter opposition against which the

Christians of the first century struggled, or to measure the courage with which they laid siege to the monstrous evils of their world. The animosity of the Jews, the ruthlessness of the empire, the viciousness of the forces of evil against which they arrayed themselves, the gulf that was fixed between them and the world they were attempting to overthrow, the overwhelming might of the paganism against which those preachers of Christ pitted their strength—all this we can appreciate but vaguely. But to their intrepidity we owe whatever we have today of spiritual assurance, and they in turn owed their faith to the fact that a divine touch had fallen upon their souls. Something holy and transforming had been imported into their lives. It was not that they had reasoned their way through to an airtight theology but that they had "faithed" their way through to a spiritual experience which had made new men of them. "Woe is unto me," one of them cried, "if I preach not the gospel!" [48] And with shouting and singing in their hearts they threw themselves with glorious abandon against the wickedness of their day, confident that in the resurrection of Jesus of Nazareth they had a word that would change the world.

v

The Apostle to the Gentiles

Dire threats from the empire, however, were not the only hazards the infant Church was compelled to face during those early years. Even more serious, in some respects, than Roman terrorism from without were the controversies which developed within the Christian movement.

It is extremely unfortunate, from the modern point of view, that our knowledge of the events of the first few decades of

Christian history is confined to such information as we are able to glean from the report of a single historian. No contemporary Roman writer, so far as we know, ever took the trouble to record the rise of the Church, or chronicle the life of any of those first great leaders of the movement. All we know, then, comes from the account prepared by a Christian who was admittedly writing from the standpoint of one friendly to the new faith and eager to see it accepted by all men everywhere.[49] It was inevitable that such a person would take pains to set forth any situation in the most favorable light possible, that the good name of the Church might not suffer.

In spite of the friendliness of the reporter, and in spite of his eagerness to portray the Christian movement in the most attractive manner, it is possible to detect evidences of violent controversies which raged inside the Christian movement, in which powerful personalities were involved, and in which vast issues were at stake. It is a mistake to assume that those first years within the fellowship were all sweetness and light.

The preacher of the word must never allow himself to forget that Christianity appeared first as a Jewish religious movement inside orthodox Judaism. Its founder, Jesus, was himself a Jewish villager who was never, with a possible single brief exception,[50] outside of Palestine. On only one occasion is it reported that he ever preached to others than Jews,[51] and even in that instance there is at least some good reason to believe that the persons referred to may have been Hellenistic Jews who had adopted the Greek life, language, and manners, but who were actually members of the Jewish race. The first Christians were all Jews; the first Christian church was organized in Jerusalem; the first missionaries went out to preach to the Jews who were scattered throughout the world.

Six hundred years of suffering for their faith had made the Jews extremely sensitive on the subject of orthodoxy. Every devout child of Abraham held, as his most profound conviction, the belief that whatever God proposed to do for the world, he proposed to do *through the Jewish nation.* To the Jews he had given the Law, which, according to their belief, contained a full and sufficient revelation of the mind and will of God for all mankind. By it all men could be saved and become the beneficiaries of his grace if they were willing to submit themselves to its requirements. This meant, of course, that all seekers after salvation must first of all become Jews, since none but Jews were eligible to salvation. As a result of this belief the Jews were engaged in a missionary enterprise which was making vigorous efforts throughout the entire East to convert the Gentiles to Judaism. This endeavor was meeting with very considerable success, so that there was a growing hope inside Judaism that the day of final triumph might actually be on its way at last.

In one matter, however, the Jews were very positive. *Every convert who sought the benefits of God's promises to the Jews must first of all become a Jew.* To do so he must go through certain ceremonies and submit to the ritual of circumcision. There could be no exceptions or deviations.

The question of the admission of Gentiles into its fellowship arose very early in the experience of the Christian Church. This was inevitable for the simple reason that, within the space of a few weeks following the resurrection of Jesus, thousands of pious pilgrims in Jerusalem had heard the story and were on their way to their homes in distant parts of the world convinced of its truthfulness.[52] No report so amazing could long be confined to even so exclusive a people as the Jews, and devout men of many races began inquiring concerning the matter. Having heard, they believed and applied for membership in the fellowship, thus bringing the matter of circumcision into sharp relief. The question the Christians faced was very simple: *"Must a Gentile who would become a Christian first become a Jew?"* Around that issue the controversy raged.

When the storm first broke inside the Jerusalem church, which was, to all intents and purposes, the governing body among the Christians, it involved two great Christian leaders. Peter, the acknowledged leader of the original band of twelve disciples, adhered to the traditional Jewish position, arguing that God's benefits were originally promised to the Jews and that any Christian, of whatever race he might be, must first of all become a Jew and after that a Christian. Ranged against him in the matter was a Hellenist Jew from the city of Tarsus, who had gone in his youth by the name of Saul, but who was later known among the Christians by the name of Paul. Both were giants in the faith.

Born in the great Roman metropolis of Tarsus, one of the dominant commercial centers of the ancient East, Paul had been schooled according to the best university standards of the time.[53] His father had been granted Roman citizenship for some conspicuous service to the empire, the exact nature of which is unknown, as a result of which he enjoyed all the privileges of a Roman freeman,[54] a fact of which he was not a little proud,[55] and also a fact of very great value to him on occasions.[56]

Having been born outside of Palestine, having been educated at least in part according to Greek standards, and speaking the Greek language with some fluency, Paul represented the better element among the Hellenist Jews. He was, how-

ever, a member of the strictest sect among the Jews—a Pharisee
—and when first we meet him in the Christian record, he
was a leader in the persecutions of the Christians. In a spectacular conversion, however, he was turned about, and from
being a relentless pursuer of the Christians he became a
preacher of the faith.[57]

As a Hellenist Jew Paul was a matchless pleader of the
cause; as a Roman citizen he had free access to every corner
of the empire; as a scholar in the field of Greek learning he
was capable of preaching the gospel to the critical and the
learned. In a word, he was apostleship at its best.

It was an age of travel, with Roman roads linking all cities
and lands into one grand whole. Seldom in history has the
world been so nearly united. A universal language, a common
code of law, and a unified political control over all of life produced a remarkable uniformity among all peoples. There remained only the need for a universal faith to bind the souls
of men together, and this the Christians were able to supply.
At first they groped their way, scarcely realizing the full meaning of their message. They have been given credit for having
turned the world upside down,[58] but actually they did nothing
more than go about telling the story of one who had been dead
but had risen from the grave and been seen alive among men.

Occasionally there appeared among the Christians a scholar
like Apollos the Alexandrian,[59] whose great learning and pol-
ished speech and manners lent prestige to the message. Many
years later than the time of which we write, one of the greatest minds of all religious history—a certain John, living in
Ephesus—arose to grapple with profound philosophical problems which were raised by the life and person of Jesus. But
those first Christian preachers for the most part were nonpro-

fessionals who had been gripped by a great fact, who had lived through a profound spiritual experience, and who were driven by a powerful inner compulsion to tell the news to anyone who could be persuaded to listen.

It was inevitable, however, that a story fraught with such tremendous meaning as was the report of Jesus' resurrection would, sooner or later, spill over into the Gentile world. And that was exactly what happened.

The Apostle Paul, in company with certain older Christians, had gone on a preaching tour in the course of which he visited a number of the more important cities of the province of Galatia. It may have been his cosmopolitan approach, it may have been the widespread spiritual hunger, or it may have been that rumors of the Resurrection had gone on ahead of the preachers. At any rate, he found himself preaching to numerous non-Jews, and before long some of these presented themselves as candidates for membership in the Christian Church. No sooner did word of this unexpected success reach the Jerusalem church than some of the more strict-minded became alarmed and managed to have preachers sent to Antioch, where Paul and his companions had returned, to make sure that they were having the new converts submit to the Jewish ritual of circumcision. This precipitated the crisis.

At first the Jerusalem preachers engaged the evangelists in a hot debate on the subject.[60] Then the issue was carried to Jerusalem, and a meeting of the church council was called to hear the matter at length. The two reports of the conference which remain to us [61] give somewhat varying accounts of what actually happened. In one Peter is represented as having acted as a mediator, but in Paul's own letter to the Galatians there is more than a hint that between him and Peter the argument was vigorous and prolonged. But whatever those facts may have been, it is agreed that Paul was given complete freedom to go back to the Gentile world and preach the Christian gospel.[62]

While engaged in a preaching mission in the city of Troas,[63] one of the important coastal towns of Asia, the apostle experienced a vision in which there appeared to him a man from Macedonia—a European—who implored him to come over and preach the gospel to the Gentiles. Convinced that he was being divinely guided, and bearing the commission of the Jerusalem church, Paul set out and was soon thereafter engaged in the enterprise. There are those who believe it likely that he was taken ill in Troas, for he is known to have suffered from some serious chronic ailment, and that in seeking relief he engaged the services of Luke, a young Greek physician. There is a rather broad hint that the youthful doctor was himself the man of the dream, for he seems to have had Macedonian connections, and we know that from this point on the story as it appears in the book of Acts uses the pronoun "we," indicating that the writer was himself a member of the apostle's party.

Emancipated from the necessity of conforming to the strict Jewish ritual, and left free to appeal to the moral conscience and spiritual hunger of the Gentile world, the Christian movement began to spread. Like some divinely driven spirit Paul hurried from city to city across the known world, preaching, evangelizing, planting churches, instructing believers, and setting in motion tides of religious fervor that began to shake the foundations of paganism. These, in turn, incited the opposition of the Jews, who looked upon the Christians as their spiritual enemies, with the result that persecution, terrorism, and conflict became the order of the day for the believers. Meanwhile the movement grew, and thousands flocked to join Christian churches.

Even smooth roads, however, could not take the terrible fatigue out of long journeys. It was a primitive age at best, and more even than courage was required to persuade a preacher to take to the highways. To be a Christian evangelist required that a man be driven by a burning passion which consumed all other interests. Paul has left us a particularly intimate account of the difficulties he had to endure as a herald of the word. Five times he was lashed by the Jews, three times he was beaten with rods, once he was stoned, and three times he suffered shipwreck. On at least one occasion he battled for his life through a terrifying day and night in the deep, clinging to a bit of driftwood. In perils by sea, from robbers, at the hands of the Jews, at the mercy of the heathen, in the desert, weary, sick, bruised and wounded, hungry, cold, stripped, betrayed [64]—"But," he wrote with the exultation of a great triumph within his soul, "none of these things move me." Of such was the mettle of those first preachers whose example we have inherited and whose word we are commissioned to preach.

In Paul's preaching there were two constantly recurring themes: the death and the resurrection of Jesus. Upon the meaning of his death and upon the fact of his resurrection he based his entire ministry. To the Corinthians he said, "I determined not to know anything among you, save Jesus Christ, and him crucified." [65] Again later he wrote, "And if Christ be not raised, your faith is vain." [66]

The very urgency under which the great apostle labored

was such that he never paused long enough to formulate his theology in orderly form. It is rather impressive that, though we know more about his mind and his Christian concepts than we do about those of any other Christian of the first century, it is impossible to reduce his teachings to systematic form. In spite of the fact that such remnants of his correspondence as remain to us reveal him as a man with a massive mind, he never seems to have put his thinking down in any completely logical form. He was primarily an administrator rather than a theologian.

Never, perhaps, in all the history of religion has a great spiritual concept been so completely trusted to the keeping of the common people as was Christianity when it was preached to the Roman world of the first century. Seldom did any church enjoy the advantages of trained or skilled leadership for more than a few weeks or months at a time. Paul's prolonged stay with the Corinthians and his slightly longer residence in Ephesus constituted the longest pastorates on record. The case of the church at Thessalonica is especially notable. There, in the midst of the starkest paganism, Paul preached for a period of no more than a few weeks before bitter persecution drove him from the city. Yet his converts, barely out of the crudest sort of heathenism, held out solidly against threats, inconveniences, oppression, and possible tortures, and became one of the most firmly established churches on the continent! One brief visit from the apostle did it! Plain people demonstrated their ability to comprehend the faith and live transformed lives. The gospel, meanwhile, showed its capacity to take root in even the most unpromising soil, and to bear fruitage in redeemed lives which astonished the world.

When the Jerusalem church, in disposing of a troublesome theological problem, commissioned Paul as the apostle to the Gentiles,[67] it served the cause of Christianity better than it knew. From that day forward every Gentile church became his personal responsibility, and the spiritual welfare of every Gentile Christian became a charge against his time, his prayers, and his strength.

Paul's mind was one of those inclusive intellects which takes in worlds. At one time he had under consideration a vast missionary enterprise by which far distant lands, out at the fringes of civilization, were to be evangelized. Only his imprisonment prevented him from carrying it into execution. At all times he carried upon his heart the needs of Christians everywhere, and his churches became the subject of his daily prayers and intercessions. In administering the affairs of the Christian movement in the Gentile world he became one of the greatest letter writers in history. It is doubtful if we have as many personal communications from the hand of any other person who ever lived in antiquity as we have from the pen of the Apostle Paul. *And his private correspondence became scripture*, so that today, from hundreds of thousands of Christian pulpits, trained and scholarly men arise to explain to waiting congregations what he said and meant. There is no greater miracle in all the spiritual records of the race.

Any man who rises on the Sabbath day to "preach the word" is apt to find himself turning almost instinctively to the letters of Paul the apostle. Next to the actual sayings of Jesus, the words of the Hellenist Jew who was a Roman citizen and became a Christian apostle have furnished more spiritual guidance to men than have the religious teachings of any other man who ever lived. Yet, strange to say, everything Paul ever said about God, life, or salvation which has any modern value stems from a single experience which he had along a dusty highway leading from Jerusalem up to Damascus.

It happened while he was yet a youth.

As a fanatical young Jew, consumed with a passionate devotion to Judaism, and to that extent profoundly religious, Paul persecuted the Christians. His terrible zeal made his name a synonym for terror among the believers, so that even Christians in distant cities shuddered at its mere mention.

Securing from the Jerusalem authorities a commission by which he was ordained to go to Damascus, in Syria, and there begin a crusade against the infant Church, Paul set out on his way, a relentless soul with but a single purpose. Christianity must be extirpated, even if it became necessary to kill the last Christian.

Somewhere along the way, while he journeyed, the young zealot was overtaken by a vision. There is some confusion in the account concerning the details, but there is no confusion concerning the result. The persecutor was subdued; the zealot was transformed; the fanatic was redeemed. He entered the city of Damascus, not as a slaughterer of the believers, but as a humbled spirit seeking the way in complete sincerity and utter honesty. Years afterward, when he was on trial for his life, he explained the rerouting of his career in a single simple statement: "Whereupon, O king Agrippa, I was not disobedient unto the heavenly vision." [68]

That doctrine of the personal vision of God—the inner conviction that one has heard the voice of God—remains to this day the basic theme for all those who would preach the word. As long as the Christian preacher is able to convince his hearers that he has been in personal communication with the

Most High, he may be sure of a reverent and respectful hearing. Down through the centuries the Christian Church has made its greatest progress during those periods when its preachers have left the least doubt in the minds of the people that God was speaking through their voices.

An aged caretaker was standing just outside the door of a church one morning when the preacher arrived. Within the space of a few minutes the minister would be standing in his pulpit leading the people in their search for God. As the old janitor straightened up to greet him, he said: "Good morning, pastor. *Any late news from God this morning?*"

And with that challenge ringing in his ears the clergyman went on into his pulpit.

Preach the word!

Any late news from God this morning?

The apostles had it!

VI

The Passion Narrative

Modern scholarship has opened up for us a very vivid New Testament. We now know some of the processes by which it came into its present form. Research has robbed it of much of its mystery, and its characters now walk among us as flesh-and-blood human beings who spent their lives with passion and enthusiasm in behalf of a hope which they believed would usher in the triumph of the will of God. Cut into it anywhere today and it will bleed.

More even than the discovery of its sheer humanity, we have discovered its sublime sanctity. The longer we probe among its origins, the more we are convinced that only by the power and guidance of the Holy Spirit of the living God could it have come into existence.

It is highly important to our work as good ministers of Jesus Christ, intent upon preaching the word, that we should adjust our minds at the outset to one extremely important fact. Let us not be deceived by the simplicity with which it can be stated. *The New Testament was produced by a new spiritual experience of God which was shared by thousands of persons throughout the ancient East.*

On the day the Galilean preacher arrived in Ephesus to proclaim the news of the risen Jesus, there was not a line of Christian literature in existence. The inspired men who raced across the earth proclaiming the news, "He is risen! He is alive!" were too busy to write down any records. Such news cannot wait; it must be told. Moreover, they had no thought that there was any need of any written records. They had already witnessed one miracle in which the prophet had broken forth from the tomb, and the faith grew up among them that another might occur at any moment by which he would return and walk the ways of men with them again. It was admitted by even his most enthusiastic admirers that he had not done the complete work of the Messiah upon the occasion of his first life among men; and, having seen him rise from the grave, they could not doubt that he was capable of returning for a second life in which his messianic work would be completed. All this had the effect of producing a mighty sense of expectancy. Anything could happen at any time, and men do not write much under those circumstances.

By the very nature of the case all Christians looked to Jesus as their final authority in conduct and experience. Not only was he their hope of heaven, but likewise he was their guide for life. The fact of the Resurrection invested even the most minute details of his life and conversation with new significance. One can well afford to ponder with care the words of a man who has been dead and is alive again. What such a one has to say about money, divorce, God, morals, mercy, sex, brotherhood, or peace cannot be ignored except at the peril of our souls.

That the Church faced bewildering problems goes without saying. The moral code of the Christians called for an entirely new type of conduct; the mystery of the Resurrection itself demanded that discerning minds should explain what manner of man Jesus was; the intimate and delicate social relationships of the times called for a new evaluation of questions of right and wrong.

As answers to such questions the Christians had memories of the Master's words. Sometimes it was a story he had told which illustrated an ideal; in other instances it was a brilliant bit of counsel given in a private conversation; in still other cases it was a fragment of a sermon he had preached. But scattered about among the Christians was a body of teachings from the lips of the prophet which served now to guide his followers in "the way."

Spread as they were throughout the empire, these sayings, stories, and reports naturally developed minor divergencies as they circulated in different areas. In Ephesus, for instance, there were considerable numbers of devout men who continued to believe that John the Baptist had been the Messiah of the Jews.[69] In Rome there appear to have been none such. When the Christian message took written form in Ephesus (the Fourth Gospel), it was inevitable that it would take the Johnite movement into account, that it would explain the difference between the two great preachers, and that it would show their relationship one to the other. But when the Gospel took written form in Rome (Mark's Gospel), it would not be necessary to deal with this problem, for there were no Johnites in that city to raise the issue.

Social and moral conditions in the great Christian centers —Jerusalem, Antioch, Ephesus, and Rome—varied considerably. The question of divorce, for instance, presented problems in Antioch which did not appear in Jerusalem, which may explain why Matthew's Gospel—which originated, apparently, in Antioch—gives more attention to this problem than any of the other three Gospels. Similar differences, usually quite slight, seem to have appeared in the accounts of miracles, the reports of parables, and the records of particular activities of the Master.

The simple truth is that for many years the Church generally preferred the oral tradition to the written record. Even as late as A.D. 130 the venerable Papias records the fact that he found the gospel which circulated by word of mouth from one Christian to another very much more satisfactory than anything that had been written down on paper, and both Paul [70] and Luke [71] admit that they depended upon the oral traditions in a large way.

It may come as something of a surprise to the modern man, accustomed as he is to relying upon written records for all important facts, to discover this ancient distrust of literary material; but the historians make it perfectly plain that such a skepticism did exist among those first-century Christians. The written word of the apostles, upon which we place our entire reliance, had to win its way against an opposition that surrendered reluctantly.

It is of very great significance, therefore, that there should be widespread agreement among modern scholars, based upon all the evidence now available, that the passion narrative, the story of the death and resurrection of Jesus, seems to have been the first portion of the Christian gospel to have been put into written form. The two great facts in the Christian faith—the death and resurrection of Jesus—upon which the entire movement rested, apparently formed the nucleus of a document that must have circulated rather widely among the Christians. Certainly it was the core of the first written Gospel.[72]

All this indicates one towering truth: *The Christian Church of the Apostolic Age rested its case on the Resurrection.*

As the Christian preacher stood that day in the Ephesus market place, he was made courageous in his attack on the city's mind and morality by the fact that death, unable to silence his Master, would be powerless to make any effective attack on him. His was more than a serene confidence in the hope of personal immortality. He was made absolutely fearless in the presence of wickedness by an assurance that the truth he spoke could never be vanquished, that it would ultimately overcome the world. And that serenity rested on the Resurrection. "Because he lives," he said, "I too shall live." It is not surprising, therefore, that hard-pressed Christian preachers exclaimed, "Thanks be to God, which giveth us the victory through our Lord, Jesus Christ." [73]

VII

The Resurrection Was the Beginning

What has already been suggested, we now repeat: *The resurrection of Jesus produced the Christian Church.* The story of Jesus Christ who was raised from the dead was the word with which the apostles defeated paganism.

Let any man who would "preach the word" ponder this fact with the utmost diligence. It was not what Jesus had to say about brotherhood, war, social relationships, or spiritual principles that laid paganism low. Other preachers had taught the people better ways of living than they were practicing, *but Jesus was the only one of them all who ever rose from the dead.* It was the Resurrection which made important whatever Jesus said about God, man, morality, or social problems.

Other prophets had been martyred; other great minds had pronounced judgment upon the iniquities of the world; other sensitive souls had proclaimed human rights and demanded justice; Jesus did all this and then, when death interrupted his message, he arose and went on with his work as though nothing had happened.

Throughout the world, and especially among the Jews, there was a vague but persistent hope that the future might be better than the present. The human soul instinctively revolted against the sight of thirty thousand men being auctioned off to the highest bidder on a Roman battlefield, to spend the rest of their days as slaves. Rome's benefits were many, and the *pax Romana* had been a vast blessing to the earth, but there was a blind groping after liberty, justice, righteousness, and the sanctities of life which could not be satisfied with even great Caesar's largess.

The resurrection of Jesus made all this blind groping and persistent hoping seem reasonable. Something of the disaster which might have followed his death if he had not been raised from the dead may be guessed from a single comment of one of the unnamed disciples who trudged his weary way back to Emmaus with leaden feet before it was known that the Master was alive. "We trusted," he said, "that it had been he which should have redeemed Israel." [74] The heavy heel of Rome, the stern discipline of the Jewish ceremonial law, the sterility of the temple worship, the complete hopelessness of any Jewish political aspiration, and the vapid faith generated by the doctors of the Law had produced an unutterable longing which they could not satisfy, and the prophet of Galilee had seemed to assure them that such longings were not in vain. But when he was laid, dead, in the rock tomb of Joseph of Arimathaea, the hope died.

Then the news of the Resurrection brought that hope to life again! The living Christ proclaimed the fact that evil does not have the last word in our world. *That word belongs to God!*

From the first announcement that he was risen all of life became invested with a new significance. God, not Caesar, became the world's center; righteousness, not evil, was eternal.

The thing that happened in the market place in Ephesus that day under the impassioned preaching of the Christian was happening all over the world. As soon as men believed that Jesus Christ had been raised from the dead and was alive again, they turned to his words with a desperate earnestness. "Surely," they reasoned, "this man who conquered death can tell us how to conquer besetments, fears, anxieties, life itself." Everything he had ever said took on importance. One whom God would not permit to die must have been one who had spoken words of truth and soberness.

That first Christian preacher was only the first of many who stood in the market place of Ephesus and told the story, for a succession of others came that way during the next twenty years. Merchants, driving trains of asses laden with merchandise, paused long enough in the bazaars to declare their faith in the story. Slaves passed the word about among their kind. Wandering workingmen, in search of employment, discussed the matter with their fellow workers while they waited for some employer in need of their services. In time, the exact date and circumstances being uncertain, there was a little group of sincere seekers in Ephesus who, believing the report, began to meet with some regularity on the evening of the first day of the week to commemorate the Master's triumph over death. At first it was only a community of believers, but as their numbers grew, a simple organization was perfected, and they called themselves a church. The word of the apostles was bearing fruit.

Out of those two great Christian facts—the death and resurrection of Jesus—came a theology. Having believed in these twin marvels, Christians found it necessary to explain the Master. Doctrines of the Atonement, the Incarnation, the pre-existent Christ, the witness of the Spirit, and forgiveness of sin through divine grace appeared, growing out of the life-giving soil of that tremendous revelation of God when he assumed the form of a man and lived among us. The preacher of the word must never forget, however, that these great Christian doctrines were all the by-products of the fact of the Resurrection. The Church would never have felt under any necessity of explaining Jesus if he had not arisen from the grave. Even the crucified raise no questions if they continue dead.

Whatever gospel we have to preach, *if it is the gospel,* rests upon the fact of the Resurrection. If we stand in our pulpits and assure men that forgiveness awaits them in the heart of

God, then the worth of that promise depends upon the fact of the Resurrection. Only one who enjoyed the favor of the Father and was raised from the dead has any authority to make such a promise. What is commonly called the "personal gospel" is no gospel at all except that it draws its validity from the great central fact of the Christian faith. If, on the other hand, we preach what is sometimes called the "social gospel," then its redemptive power depends upon the Resurrection. The gospel of the kingdom of heaven which Jesus preached is justified on only one condition—that the preacher thereof was of God. And this, in Jesus' case, was proved by the empty tomb. Only he who has defeated death is capable of defeating the evil of this world.

Volumes have been written on the faith of the fathers, but the substance of that faith has never been better expressed than by Paul, the greatest of the apostles, when he said, *"If Christ be not risen, then is our preaching vain."* [75]

If any man would "preach the word," then let him preach the resurrection of Jesus of Nazareth, for this was the word of the apostles.

the Word... OF THE BELIEVERS

I
Antipas of Pergamos

If only someone had thought to preserve for us the story of Antipas of Pergamos! We know so little about him, and yet he is so important a link in the chain of the story.

Was he one of those who fought barehanded with wild beasts in the stadium to provide entertainment for the jaded spirits of bloody Romans? Or was he one of those heroic souls who, rather than recant their faith, gave their bodies to be burned as living, blazing torches in the garden of the emperor?

We will never know. All we can be absolutely sure of is that he is mentioned as having been one of that regal company of the faithful who counted not their lives dear unto themselves, and became living sacrifices in the Christian cause, believing it to be their reasonable service.[76]

A trifle would have saved Antipas. All that was required of him was that he should pronounce the words "Domitian, lord and god," before the imperial altar in Pergamos. Had he done so, Caesar would have been satisfied. But this he steadfastly refused to do.

The Romans were never able to understand him, but that was because neither they nor any others without deep religious convictions have ever been able to understand any man to whom a religious faith is something holy and possessive. Having no profound convictions of their own, they were unable to comprehend the mind of a man who held many things supremely sacred.

The times had become extremely dangerous for Christians. As far back as the days of Caesar Augustus there had been those who, thinking they were flattering the emperor, had erected a magnificent temple in Pergamos [77] whereat prayers were offered to him and a ritual was performed which invoked his blessing as though he were a god. Augustus accepted the tribute with a certain disdainful good humor, but succeeding occupants of the throne were seduced by the implications of the ceremonies, and in time similar temples and ceremonies put in their appearance in widely separated cities of the world.

Most brazen of all the emperors, actually demanding worship from the people, was Domitian. Vain, ruthless, arrogant, intolerant, incapable of even the rudiments of mercy, he exalted the demands of the emperor cult until it would tolerate no rival. Every citizen of the empire was required to worship or go underground.

It is a little difficult for modern Christians, accustomed as they are to the operation of the principle of freedom of worship, to appreciate the problems raised for those first-century believers by the emperor cult. No man, for instance, unwilling to swear by the emperor—an acknowledgment of his divinity—was acceptable in the civil courts either as a litigant or as a witness. This meant that no Christian could look to the law to protect him in any right unless he was willing to forswear his faith and swear by the emperor. It meant that none could register legal papers, record deeds, collect unpaid bills by due process of law, seek redress for any wrong done them or any damage inflicted on their property. It meant that they could not establish membership in any of the labor guilds, obtain any employment in government service, participate in a public ceremony where demonstration or proof of their citizenship was required. They could not hold public office, accept public trust, or receive any public relief if they were in distress.

Among the pagans the emperor cult raised no problem. With them it was only a question of admitting one more divinity to their already crowded pantheon, of making room in their easy loyalties for one more god. To mumble the words "Domitian, lord and god," upon going into court, or in concert with the crowds at the games, involved no moral or spiritual sacrifice. Indeed it was no more than a polite gesture, quite without meaning or value. If such lighthearted reverence gratified the vainglorious soul of Domitian, then he was welcome to it! It cost them nothing!

Not so with the Christians, or with the Jews, for that matter. According to their belief it was not a mere matter of admitting a new god into a congested circle of deities; it was impossible for them to agree that there was any God of any sort other than the Father of their Lord Jesus Christ. The ancient Jewish faith, made solemn by countless repetitions of the affirmation through the long centuries—"Hear, O Israel: *The Lord our God is one Lord*" [78]—was extremely jealous, refusing to concede divine honors to any, not even one, beside Jehovah, the ancestral God of Israel. To the Christians unyielding belief in one God was the very core of their con-

103

viction. To offer the slightest shred of tribute to the emperor as being divine was to deny everything their faith called sacred.

Just how Antipas of Pergamos fell afoul of the law we will never know. Some suspicious citizen may have noticed that he did not stand and swear by the emperor at one of the athletic games when the herald appeared to summon the multitude to its feet—something similar to the modern salute to the flag—and hurried away forthwith to report the case to an officer of the law in the hope that such evidence of patriotic zeal might win some official favor. Or it may have been that in offering or collecting a coin bearing Caesar's image he did not mumble, "Domitian, lord and god." It may even have been that he was summoned into court to give testimony in a case concerning which he was the only living person in possession of evidence. Having refused to swear by Caesar, he found himself the accused and the defendant instead of the witness.

By an almost endless series of dangerous possibilities Antipas may have become involved, and it makes little difference by which he was tripped up. It is sufficient for our purpose that a mighty preacher of the times—a certain John, who had been a leader of the churches in the province of Asia—in an effort to arouse the loyalties of the Christians and strengthen their souls in anticipation of the terrible persecutions that were impending, cited him in a blazing book penned on Patmos as one whose faithfulness unto death was to be emulated by all. In that single reference we catch a glimpse of the tortured times through which the Christians were living about A.D. 90.

In the final analysis the acid test of any philosophy, theology, political program, social procedure, or religious faith is its effect upon the individual person. The ancient Egyptians built imposing pyramids in the hope that they would immortalize the glory of the Pharaohs, but those huge piles of masonry stand today as monuments to monsters who mixed their mortar with the blood of their slaves. The glory that was Rome was written in the sweat of a world that groaned in slavery. Every tyrant of antiquity was seated upon a throne made unsteady by the fact that it rested upon the backs of men who writhed in abject wretchedness. The glitter and the glamour of kings was a veneer spread thin, but it would not hide the horrors of those who agonized and died underneath the tinsel and the gilt.

It is by its effect upon the individuals who have accepted its teachings that Christianity is to be judged, and he who would preach the word must preach the word of the believers, men and women who gave their lives rather than recant their faith. Antipas of Pergamos has had spiritual kinsmen in every generation—heroic spirits who have not denied the faith, but who have kept the name holy. They have testified to amazing experiences within their own souls, and in the final analysis the case for Christianity must rest upon their testimonies.

The story is told of a revealing interchange between Charles Bradlaugh, the celebrated English atheist, and Hugh Price Hughes, the famous evangelist of London's mission halls. Partly for the sake of publicity, and partly for the sake of eliciting a discussion of the issue between belief and unbelief, the atheist issued a challenge to the evangelist to meet him in debate. The proposal was published in the "vox pop" column of one of London's newspapers, and included an offer on the part of Bradlaugh to hire the hall, pay the expenses, and make the necessary arrangements.

The Christian preacher hastened to accept. Using the columns of the same newspaper in which the challenge was published, the evangelist signified his entire willingness to appear and then added somewhat after this manner: "Inasmuch as I am the one challenged, I have the right to indicate at least some of the conditions under which the discussion is to be held. I am, therefore, stipulating that I shall appear at the appointed hour with one hundred men whose lives have been redeemed by believing on the Lord Jesus Christ. I will have there men who have been drunkards and are now sober, libertines whose lives have been cleansed, gamblers who have been made into honest men, wife-beaters who have become kindly homemakers. I will expect Mr. Bradlaugh to be present with another hundred men whose lives have been redeemed from evil and made righteous by the teachings to which he has dedicated his life. We will allow these men to offer their testimonies, and then we will ask the audience to judge the debate on the basis of the reports these men give of their redemptions."

At the appointed hour Hughes appeared at the hall with his hundred trophies of grace. They took their place upon the platform in full view of the vast audience that had assembled, and waited. Bradlaugh never put in an appearance. When fifteen minutes had elapsed, according to the story as it is told in London, and the evangelist and his company of redeemed men were in possession of the occasion, the preacher arose and said, "Since there seems to be no probability of a debate, I see no reason why we should not hold a meeting, and in the absence of Mr. Bradlaugh and his friends I am going to ask some of these who have accompanied me to tell you their story." With that he turned the meeting into a religious service and preached the word of salvation, supported by ringing and enthusiastic testimonies of men who could say out of experience, "I know whom I have believed!"

II
It Began with Stephen

Jerusalem was in an uproar. A shocking thing had happened. A young Hellenist Jew had been arrested for preaching strange doctrines, and when he had been brought before the Sanhedrin, he had accused the leaders of the Jews of having murdered their Messiah!

The Hellenists were always under some suspicion, however. Their cosmopolitan speech, their indifference to the ceremonial law, their familiarity with, and tolerance for, Greek learning, and their laxity in matters of ritual stigmatized them as liberals. Many of them were not even able to speak the Hebrew language. Their blood might be Jewish, for they had been born of the stock of Israel, but they were essentially Greeks, for they had been born outside Palestine, and in all matters, save those of race and religion, they had accepted the life and culture of the Greek world. All this had the effect of making them a bit disdainful in the face of the contempt of the temple aristocracy. Though they paid their temple tax of a half shekel meticulously, it was impossible for them to observe the multitudinous forms and regulations required of a strict Hebrew of the Hebrews.

The difficulty in which the young Hellenist had become involved occurred at the Synagogue of the Libertines,[79] a house of worship provided especially for the accommodation of the foreign-speaking Jews in Jerusalem. What had started off as a sober discussion of the tenets of the new sect which

had appeared among the Jews developed into something resembling a riot. There were among the Hellenists occasional
individuals who undertook to compensate for their separation
from the privileges of the temple with a fanatical devotion to
orthodoxy. These were often more Jewish than the Jews of
Jerusalem, and certain of their number precipitated an unseemly proceeding with the result that serious charges were
carried to the high priest.

Stephen, the young Hellenist against whom the charges
were made, was by all accounts a remarkable young man. His
face was fascinating in its beauty, and his spirit was ordinarily
as gentle as that of a dove. But he had been profoundly moved
by the story he heard concerning the crucifixion of Jesus of
Nazareth, and as he opened his mind to it, a change had
come over his life that was little less than miraculous. He
continued to retain his gentleness of spirit, but the firmness
with which he believed that Jesus was the Messiah of the
Jews produced in him a courage and forthrightness that was
magnificent.

It was true, the prophet had been crucified. No one attempted to deny that. And it was also true that the temple
authorities had persuaded the Roman procurator to pass the
death sentence. In that the hierarchy took a certain grim
satisfaction, for they persuaded themselves that they had been
defending the faith of their fathers in doing so. That they had
also been defending their personal revenues was not mentioned. At any rate, orthodoxy had spoken, and that should
have settled the matter. But it did not.

The disciples of the prophet declared that their Master had
broken forth from the grave on the morning of the second
day following his entombment, and that he was alive and

present with them. They had persuaded a considerable company to believe their tale, as many as three thousand having declared their faith in Jesus at one meeting.

All this might have been passed over in silence by the temple authorities if a new element had not entered the situation. Those who believed in the risen prophet declared that he had been the Messiah of the Jews, and that he had been crucified by the very ones—the high priest and his colleagues—who should have been first to recognize his divine character and mission. This was much more serious than it appears to a modern Christian, to whom the peculiar covenant between God and the Jews has small meaning. But the alert doctors of the Law were quick to see its implications. It meant, in simple terms, that if the disciples of the crucified prophet were allowed to continue making the claim that Jesus was the Messiah of the Jews, then his followers became the true Israel, and all those who rejected his messianic claims were apostates. This clearly contained all the elements of a major crisis in the nation's life.

So assiduous were the preachers of the new sect in promoting their beliefs that the situation was fast getting out of hand, and it all headed up in the Synagogue of the Libertines, with Stephen, the Hellenist, one of the ringleaders.

Rather curiously, the whole matter had never had an official hearing, and the Sanhedrin had never had an opportunity to pass its judgment. The riot at the Synagogue of the Libertines, however, provided just such an opportunity, and Stephen was hailed into court and required to state his case. He did so in a dignified and winsome manner and was clearly making a very favorable impression until he came to the point where he assessed the blame for the death of Jesus. Then he became almost blunt. In the plainest possible words he laid the charge at the door of the leaders of the Jews—*they had crucified the Lord's anointed and the nation's hope.*

Those who are professionally religious are seldom entirely patient with theological amateurs. As long as the people are willing to follow their leaders without asking questions, all goes well; but when men begin thinking independently, someone is very likely to begin making ready for a stoning. It was so in Jerusalem that day when Stephen, the Hellenist become Christian, addressed the Jewish Sanhedrin.

The address which the young man delivered must have been a model of passion and logic. The record we have in the New Testament in the book of Acts gives no more than the basic theme; and that, we must remember, cannot have been gleaned from any stenographic report, for, so far as we know, no friends of the young man were permitted to be present in the court to hear the charges against him or his defense. Luke, the immortal historian of those first years of the Christian Church, was compelled to piece the story together out of materials gathered from a variety of sources, and there is undoubtedly very much of Luke himself in it as we now have it in the New Testament. But at least we know the major facts. Stephen was stoned to death, and became the first martyr to die for his faith in the risen Jesus.

Lest anyone should be disturbed by the fact that we must confess Luke's account of Stephen's address is not a verbatim record from an eyewitness, let us hasten to remind ourselves that *Luke was himself a believer*, and his account of Stephen's speech as it appears in his Acts of the Apostles represents not only the convictions of the young Hellenist but also the profoundest convictions of a devout Greek Christian who wrote at least half a century afterward. What Luke reports Stephen as having said, Luke would have said had he himself been on trial.

Perhaps it will help us just a bit at this point to pause for a moment and get acquainted with Luke too. His name indicates that he was a Greek, and the book of Acts reveals him as a trained physician converted from paganism to Christianity under the preaching of the Apostle Paul, the greatest of all that generation of first-century Christian preachers. As Paul's traveling companion through many years Luke had exceptional opportunities to gather firsthand information concerning the rise of the Christian Church, and his two-volume history (Luke and Acts) bears evidence that he was a historian of remarkable ability and a literary artist of the first rank. Renan, the great French critic and skeptic, has called Luke's Gospel "the most beautiful book ever written."

Much more impressive, however, than any of his professional talents and skills—and they are admittedly great—were the fixedness of his belief in the essential deity of the prophet of Galilee and his sublime confidence in the truth of the resurrection story which he tells in detail in his book. No one who ever lived has been a more convinced believer in the Christian faith than the Greek physician who became Paul's traveling companion.

As we read the Gospel of Luke and the book of Acts, we must bear in mind the fact that both were written many years after the events they describe. In the meantime the Christian message, and the story of the life and teachings of the prophet of Galilee, had been subjected to the most careful scrutiny.

111

Every detail of the oral tradition had been examined by all those living who had come in contact in any way with the living Jesus. Numerous written records of one kind and another had come into existence and circulated among the people. These, like the oral traditions, had been scanned by those who had firsthand knowledge. What Luke wrote, therefore, represents the matured judgment of a trained mind, the research of a scientific observer, and the faith of an enlightened soul who wrote out of a rich spiritual experience. Moreover we must not forget that he had lived long years in the company of Paul, the greatest apostle of them all. Therefore, whatever of Luke there may be in the long speeches found in the Third Gospel and the book of Acts may be accepted as a validated portion of the true word of the apostles.

In one of his sermons Jesus had told his disciples that they were the salt which was destined to save the world from corruption and decay, and the sentence of death which the Sanhedrin inflicted upon the young Hellenist, Stephen, was the first move officialdom made to scatter the salt.

According to the laws of the Jews, one who was guilty of blasphemy was to be put to death by stoning, and the infuriated Sanhedrinists and their rowdy colleagues became almost fanatical in their hatred of the young man. His serenity angered them as much as his severity, and they dragged him from the city, set upon him like madmen, and buried him under an avalanche of stones. As the heap grew and his life was fast ebbing away, he gasped out one last prayer, *"Lord Jesus, receive my spirit; lay not this sin to their charge."* [80] Like his Master, Stephen paid with his life for his conviction; and, again like his Master, he loved his executioners to the end.

112

III
The Salt Is Scattered

The stoning of Stephen became the signal for a general exodus of all Christians from Jerusalem.[81] Only the apostles tarried in the city, but wherever the refugees went they became flaming evangelists, declaring their faith in Jesus of Nazareth and telling the amazing story of the Resurrection. The preacher who appeared that spring day in the market place of Ephesus may have been one of those who had fled for his life from the city of Jerusalem. Of course some years had elapsed between the time of Stephen's stoning and the preaching of that first Christian sermon in Ephesus, but they had been years which had seen believers strengthened in their convictions and matured in their thinking.

Christianity had become a religion of the Spirit. The believers were convinced that something holy had happened to them; they were sure they had heard the voice of the Most High God speaking to them, counseling, inspiring, guiding, warning, rebuking, enlightening. And they were heard with eagerness by the thoughtful of the world, for anyone who could speak a confident word in such a time of uncertainty was sure to get a hearing. Every Christian believer declared, "I *know* whom I have *believed*," and as a consequence all were accorded a hearing that was both respectful and wistful.

Just because the new faith was a religion of the Spirit it made an intimate appeal to the mystical mind of the Greeks. In sharp contrast to the mystery religions of that day, as well as most of the pagan faiths, Christianity required no forms or ceremonies. Its creed was extremely simple. The convert was required to make but a single affirmation of faith, and this he

113

did by saying in the presence of the congregation, "Jesus is Lord." [82] The initiatory rite of baptism, equally simple, was one in common use in civil as well as political ceremonies of the time. On the evening of the first day of the week, following the Jewish Sabbath, the Christians came together for a memorial meal to commemorate the resurrection of Jesus, each one bringing his own food and drink. In time the Christians took over the entire day and made it their holy Sabbath, but at first the observance was restricted to the evening hour. Around the tables, in worship and hospitality, they developed their fellowship, but it was their common belief which bound them together in one body.

The most significant thing about those believers, however, was the fact that they were transformed men. Their pagan neighbors often remarked, "See how those Christians love one another." Because of this, and because of the superior quality of the lives they lived, they were called "the people of the way." [83]

In every city of the empire the Christians outlived their pagan neighbors. That is, they lived on a higher moral level and enjoyed superior satisfactions in life. There was a serenity and peace within them which set paganism to wondering. They were able to rejoice in tribulation; they did not seem to count even their lives if their cause was in jeopardy; they had discovered how to live with abandon, and no one has really lived who has not lived in that fashion. They could not be terrified out of their convictions; and if, perchance, the malice or suspicion of their neighbors caused them to be thrust into jail, they spent the period of their incarceration singing and praising God.

It was not mere bravado. They were men who lived upon

the vitality of an amazing personal religious experience. Because they believed in Jesus Christ, in his resurrection, and in the faith that he was truly the Son of God, they testified to a transforming presence in their lives which could have come only from God himself. It was this inner presence which became their authority for life, conduct, and faith.

Nor was it an easy faith or salvation. It called for a complete renovation of life and remolding of character. Masters were to receive their brethren in the faith as brethren of the blood; their slaves were to be accepted as brothers, and slaves once unprofitable were expected to be profitable.[84] They offered the world a peace that was beyond human understanding, but it could be achieved only by paying the cost in moral uprightness, spiritual integrity, and a willingness to join in a solidarity of fellowship.

Theirs was the power of an authenticated experience. This is the difference between the philosophy of Jesus and that of any other teacher who ever lived. The prophet of Galilee has often been compared to Socrates, and there is a certain similarity between the two in that one died upon a cross and the other drank the hemlock. But there is also this vast difference between them: though Socrates died because of the things he believed, his followers have never willingly died for their belief in the things he taught. Jesus, on the other hand, has commanded a loyalty from his followers down through the ages which has driven many of them to martyrdom. Stephen the Hellenist and Antipas of Pergamos are but two. Of the others there is a company that no man has ever counted.

Something new had come into the world. It was not a new doctrine but a new life. Men who *believed* in the risen Lord *became new men*, and without an exception they ascribed the

115

change that had been wrought in their lives to the incoming of a new and divine Spirit which had taken possession of them from the time they first declared their faith and recited the simple creed "Jesus is Lord."

In every city of the world the miracle was happening. In most places the slaves were first to listen and confess, but they soon carried the messages deep into the houses of the masters where street preachers could never hope to penetrate, and strange things began to happen. Masters began to seek spiritual guidance from their servants. Now and again some scholar or aristocrat made an open confession of his faith and, daring a storm of ridicule or worse, threw in his lot with the Christians. All in all, it was astonishing how rapidly the salt was scattered throughout the decaying world and how soon the process of preservation began.

It was all because believers went about declaring, *"We know."* Others might speculate; the Christians spoke out of personal knowledge. Like the blind boy who had been healed of his blindness and dared to declare in the very presence of the doctors of the Law, "One thing I know, that, whereas I was blind, now I see," [85] so the empire discovered that it was dealing with a movement of which every member was a world authority on at least one subject. Every man who called himself a Christian testified to a personal knowledge of God, and a personal possession of the Spirit of God.

It is hard to stop such a movement.

IV

John of Ephesus

In spite of the certainty with which men speak who have experienced a transformation of life and character, there

116

comes a time when every faith must submit its case at the bar of reason and logic. So it was with Christianity.

The Greek mind was thoroughly disciplined. Broadly tolerant and generally hospitable, it nevertheless insisted upon strict reasoning, and by the last years of the first century the believers found themselves face to face with a series of logical problems which had to be solved or their faith would lead them no further than to the dead end of the way. The religion of Jesus was compelled to justify itself before the finest intellects of the world.

It was precisely at this juncture that one of the ablest minds of that or any other century came forward as the champion of the faith—John of Ephesus.

It would be extremely interesting if we could know even a little, exactly, of this towering personality. The name is a common one in all languages and all centuries, and it is impossible to furnish exact identification at this date. There are those who believe that John was none other than the son of Zebedee and one of the apostles; but it is passing strange, if that is so, that he did not claim apostolic authority for his book (the Fourth Gospel), since such a claim would have gone far toward establishing its status. Then there are those who believe the "beloved disciple" to whom the Gospel is attributed [86] was some genteel youth who attached himself to the Master while still a lad, and who was known to the company of disciples as the beloved disciple who leaned upon the Master's bosom, and to whom Jesus had entrusted his mother during her stay in Jerusalem following the crucifixion.[87] Still others believe that the author of the Fourth Gospel was the noted preacher, John of Ephesus, whose fame had spread abroad through the Church. Since we have no sure means of identifying him, let us be content to refer to him simply as John of Ephesus, meaning that great mind who became the apologist for the Christian faith, and who preached the doctrines of the Fourth Gospel.

In spite of the lack of definite information which would demonstrate the identity of the author who bequeathed to us the Gospel of John, it is possible for us to be sure of certain facts concerning him, and these will help us to understand the peculiar contribution he made to the word which the Christian preacher of today is exhorted to preach.

Whether or not he had ever been formally schooled in Greek philosophy we do not know, but that he was generally familiar with the philosophical theories and terminology of the great masters we are perfectly sure. His was the mind of a master, dealing with a problem in which the ages have a stake, and we must take his measure from his book, for therein is the revelation of his mind—the intellect of a profound believer and a thinker who had companied with the giants.

According to the teachings of Philo, one of the greatest of the Greeks—a Hebrew by birth, and a Greek by culture— God revealed himself to man from time to time through an "out-going spirit" which the philosopher called "the Word." Among cultivated and learned Greeks who had come under the influence of Philo—and they included the best minds of that generation—"the Word" (*ho logos,* in Greek) was accepted as meaning "the active presence of God."

John of Ephesus, in making his approach to the Greek mind, desired to present Jesus as the divine Son of God, preexistent, eternal, alive, and active in the affairs of men, and for that purpose he seized on Philo's word and concept and made two mighty assertions. The first was in the finest Mosaic tradition—"In the beginning was the Word," which was to say, "In the beginning God." This majestic proposition he followed with a second, "And the Word was made flesh, and dwelt among us," by which he meant, "And God assumed the form of a man and revealed himself to us as such. We knew him, we called him by his name, we lived and walked with him, *and we beheld his glory*." Then, with almost mathematical precision, he proceeded to prove the faith of the believers in Jesus as the Son of God.

Nowhere, in or out of the Scriptures, is there a more exhaustive or compelling statement of the case for Christianity. For nineteen hundred years the best-trained minds of the Christian world have worked their way through John's great chapters, formulating doctrines, theologies, and systems of thought, and its depths have not yet been plumbed. Yet at the same time the plain man of the street can read the Gospel of John and find it the most satisfactory statement of the word of the believer within our possession; for, it must never be forgotten, John of Ephesus was, first of all, *a believer*.

It is not important that we should know which John wrote the Gospel. The book bears abundant evidence within itself that it is the solemn testimony of a great believer who had experienced a profound spiritual undergirding. His own life had been stabilized. He had thought his way through to the light. When he reported that Jesus said, "When the Comforter is come, whom I will send unto you," it meant that *the Comforter had come to John himself*. When he quoted Jesus as saying, "I am the way," it meant that he, John, *had found that way*.

Let any man who would attempt to preach the word read the Fourth Gospel again, and try to imagine it being written by a man who had not experienced the vindication of the Master's great assurances. Let him read again that forthright word, "He that heareth my word, and believeth on him that sent me, hath everlasting life," and then try to imagine such a statement being penned by a man who was not sure of it himself!

Equipped by the Creator with a massive mind, and schooled in a radiant experience, John wrote a book which has laid Jesus of Nazareth upon the world's conscience for all time. As long as the Gospel of John survives, men will have to make up their minds about Jesus because of what one believer asserted concerning him—that he was the word made flesh and dwelling among us.

v

The Word from Patmos

Deep in the Patmos quarries a white-haired old man toiled painfully under the broiling sun, lifting and tugging at huge blocks of limestone. Now and again he paused to stand erect and rest his aching muscles, and when he did so, he revealed a face so remarkable that it could never be forgotten. The focus of that fascinating countenance was in the eyes, which blazed defiantly, fearlessly, in spite of the spent body from which they looked. The horrors of a Roman prison had been quite insufficient to crush the spirit within, and the venerable old prisoner gave the impression that he was looking far beyond the horizon to the centuries yet to be.

It was backbreaking labor in the quarries, and there were many who had gone raving mad under that relentless sun. Rome had little mercy at best, and none to spare for her penal colony on Patmos. Meanwhile the sea beat upon the rocky coast with a certain callous indifference to the poor wretches who gazed out dumbly across the waves. Even a desperate man, made frantic by the lash, could see no chance for escape. Without that strange fire which burned deep within him John, the Christian, would have gone down in complete despair as did his companions in doom, but because he had a faith that would not surrender, he had survived the years, and his spirit was unbroken, though his aged body was well-nigh spent.

No one knows just how long the old man had been imprisoned on the bleak and barren isle, and no one knows how much longer he remained. As a matter of fact, very little is known of him beyond the fact that on the dreary island he penned one of the most unusual and mysterious pieces of writing that has ever found its way into religious literature.

He was of the same generation as Antipas of Pergamos, and we do not know for what offense he had been sentenced to Patmos. All we can state with complete positiveness is that it was for the crime of being a Christian. He may have been one of those who refused to swear by Caesar when he was hailed into court, or he may have been apprehended while preaching to a little company of the faithful on the evening of the first day of the week in some upper room in Ephesus. The precise charge is unimportant; John lived when everywhere in the empire it was judged a crime to be a Christian.

Those were desperate days for the disciples of the prophet of Galilee. Their unwavering faith in the fact that he was the Son of God had brought them into deadly conflict with the claims of the emperor to the honors of divinity. The reasonably comfortable conditions which had existed in the days of Paul the apostle a generation earlier had disappeared. The great apostle had counseled the Christians under his care to obey the laws of the empire, to keep out of the courts, to avoid trouble, and to show themselves good citizens,[88] all in the hope that the infant Church might be spared the horrors of a world-wide persecution, at least until it was strong enough to fend off the blows. Luke's efforts to portray the Christian movement as one that offered no threat to Rome may have postponed the struggle for a few years, but it was inevitable that the issue would be joined sooner or later. Good and evil cannot go on indefinitely together in the same world.

On Patmos, John was only one of a great host who had fallen under the terrible wrath of the empire. It was desperately dangerous everywhere in the world to be known as a Christian. No man who called Jesus Lord was safe anywhere.

To the aged man digging in the quarries of Patmos, Rome appeared to be the embodiment of all things evil. To his blazing eyes she had all the characteristics of a harlot[89] reeking with the filth of her paramours. The vague and unsatisfactory reports which filtered through to him from incoming prisoners told of congregations of Christians scattered, of burnings, crucifixions, wild orgies in the stadia, and horrors unspeakable. Clearly there was going on in the world a war to the death between the forces of righteousness and the forces of evil, with the empire the personification of all things godless.

As the old preacher gazed out across the empty wastes of the endless waves, the agonies within his broken body seemed but emblematic of the tortures with which the Church, the bride of Christ, was inflicted. Day after day, in his memory, he recited the lists of the Christians in city after city in Asia, and asked himself, "Are they still alive? Have they kept the faith?" The beloved congregations to which he had ministered in labors of love—Ephesus, Smyrna, Pergamos, Thyatira, Sardis, Philadelphia, Laodicea—had they managed to survive?

In his utter helplessness—silenced, banished, lashed—John stared out into the blackness of nights and prayed. Through what seemed like interminable hours under the pitiless sun he mingled his petitions with his labors. And in spite of all appearances and evidences of futility his faith refused to surrender, but rose phoenixlike from the horrors of his prison island and asserted its confidence that someday Rome would fall and the Church of Christ would rise in triumph.

To this day it remains a mystery how he may have contrived it, but on Patmos, under the very eye of the Roman guards with their rods and spears, the old man managed to write a letter to his fellow Christians of Asia. By other means, equally mysterious, the letter was spirited off the island by stealth, and by still other devices was circulated among the persecuted Christians for the purpose of increasing their faith and encouraging them to stand fast.

It was necessary, of course, to write in such a fashion that, if the letter should fall into the hands of the Romans, it might appear harmless and innocent. Therefore John disguised his fervid hatred of Rome under mysterious symbols. But to the Christians his message was perfectly plain, for the symbols were in common—and perhaps secret—use among them.

Frankly it must be confessed that his letter was almost avowedly seditious. At one point, writing as though he were leading a host against the wicked empire, he wrote, "Pay her back in her own coin, and give her double for what she has done. . . . In the cup she mixed for others, mix her a double draught. . . . Gloat over her, heaven! and all you people of God, apostles, and prophets, for God has avenged you upon her!" [90]

To the modern reader John's letter is extremely difficult reading, for the key to the meaning of the symbols he uses has been lost, making many of the figures meaningless to us. But the central theme is perfectly plain, and just as brave and heroic as in the day when, in some secret hiding place on Patmos, the venerable old preacher first wrote it for the encouragement of the Christians.

All of human history was his theme, the whole universe his stage; the thunders of the heavens and the roar of the seas in the grip of the storms furnished his orchestrations. Beasts, dragons, and antichrists were his actors, but it was all intended to vindicate God's government of the universe and the divine mastery over time. Written in an hour of impenetrable blackness as far as the human eye could see, it is still livid with hope. The present might be indescribably evil, but a new heaven and a new earth were on their way and would be established in God's own good time. It became the duty of Christians, therefore, to hold fast and wait. Of course nothing could be further from the truth if men were to judge by appearances, but John's letter was a mighty effort to lift the gaze of the Christians above appearances, and up to the throne of God whereon sat their Master, the risen Christ, in glorious triumph.

It is the glory of the Christian faith that it is not a slave to appearances. It lives above them. God is not with the overwhelming legions of Rome, John shouted. He is in the dungeons with the persecuted, on the rack with the tortured, amid the flames with the burning, and out in penal colonies with the seers. *And the ultimate victory is in his hands!* There is therefore but one course open to the Christians. They are to stand steadfast, and having done all, *to stand.*

It is probably safe to say that no book of the New Testament has suffered more at the hands of its pseudo friends than the book of Revelation. Fanatics, sectarians, eccentrics, mystics, and even the devout have all gone probing about among its mysterious symbolism in search of verification for their personal and peculiar doctrines, until it has become the happy hunting ground of the controversialists. But originally it was intended to do but one thing—to furnish courage for the Church at a time when it was fighting for its life.

The weaknesses of John's letter to the churches can be admitted very candidly. It is vindictive, almost ferocious at times, and calculated to steel men to the last possible effort of resistance to government. It in no wise compares, either in majesty of concept or in depth of piety, with the sublimities of the Fourth Gospel. But it is an almost incredibly brave book. And its confidence in the ultimate triumph of God has never been surpassed, even seldom equaled. *It was written by a believer who was sure of the light when there was nothing to see but blackness. For that reason it is the message of the believer to those who sit in darkness.*

To the good minister of Jesus Christ in the cathedral pulpit with the elite of a great city in the pews before him, to the preacher who stands up in a university church with the inquiring minds of youth before him, to the man who proclaims the word of Christ to the humble, the poor, the bewildered, and the beaten, the exhortation to Timothy is still in order— *Preach the word.*

And to the aid of every man who declares his faith in the risen Christ, the Son of God, the world's Redeemer, and the ultimate Master of all of life, there will come the hosts of the prophets, the scholars, the apostles, and the believers of all the centuries, chorusing the victorious refrain, *"Thanks be to God, which giveth us the victory through our Lord Jesus Christ."*

SCRIPTURE REFERENCES

1. II Timothy 4:2.
2. Luke 2:46.
3. Isaiah 6:3.
4. Micah 6:8.
5. Amos 5:14.
6. Amos 5:21–24.
7. Isaiah 53:3–5.
8. I Kings 21:1–3.
9. Luke 1:46–55.
10. Isaiah 1:10–17; 3:13–15.
11. Jeremiah 5:1–6; 6:4–6.
12. Amos 2:6; 6:4–6; 8:6; 9:1–14.
13. Micah 1:2–9; 3:1–12.
14. Hosea 6:6; 8:6; Isa. 1:13.
15. Jeremiah 8:7; Isaiah 42:1–3; 49:4; Amos 2:4.
16. Isaiah 6:1 ff.
17. Ezekiel 1:1; 8:3; 40:2.
18. Isaiah 7:1–17.
19. Amos 7:10–17.
20. Isaiah 36—39; cf. II Kings 18:13—20:19.
21. Hosea 6:4.
22. Matthew 23:37; Luke 13:34.
23. Ezekiel 33:1–7.
24. Psalm 1:6.
25. Psalm 137:4.
26. E.g., Isaiah 14:32; 31:5.
27. Jeremiah 42:12.
28. Psalm 137:5–6.
29. Ezra 10:3, 10–44.
30. II Kings 22:9–13.
31. II Kings 21:1–18.
32. II Kings 22:16.
33. Ezekiel 3:1 ff.
34. Isaiah 52:13—53:12.
35. Genesis 32:26.
36. Nehemiah 8:1 ff.
37. Acts 22:3.
38. John 1:14.
39. II Corinthians 11:9.
40. Luke 6:15; Acts 1:13.
41. Matthew 16:13–14.
42. Matthew 9:32–34.
43. Matthew 5:27–28.
44. Luke 23:8–11.
45. I Corinthians 15:6.
46. Acts 11:26.
47. Acts 21:8–9.
48. I Corinthians 9:16.
49. Luke 1:1; Acts 1:1.
50. Matthew 14:13.
51. John 12:21.
52. Acts 2:5–11.
53. Acts 22:3.
54. Acts 22:28.
55. Acts 16:37.
56. Acts 22:27–29.
57. Acts 22:14–15.
58. Acts 17:6.
59. Acts 18:24; 19:1.
60. Acts 15:1–2.

61. Acts 15:7–11; Galatians 2:11.
62. Acts 15:30.
63. Acts 16:8–11.
64. II Corinthians 11:24–27.
65. I Corinthians 2:2.
66. I Corinthians 15:17.
67. Acts 15:22–35.
68. Acts 26:19.
69. Acts 19:1–3; John 1:6–8, 15–36.
70. Galatians 6:6; Colossians 1:5; II Thessalonians 2:13.
71. Luke 1:2.
72. Mark 14—15.
73. I Corinthians 15:57.
74. Luke 24:21.
75. I Corinthians 15:14.
76. Revelation 2:13.
77. Revelation 2:12–17.
78. Deuteronomy 6:4.
79. Acts 6:9.
80. Acts 7:60.
81. Acts 8:1.
82. Acts 16:31–33.
83. Acts 19:9.
84. Philemon 11.
85. John 9:25.
86. John 19:26; 20:2.
87. John 19:27.
88. Romans 13:1–7.
89. Revelation 17:5.
90. Revelation 18:6, 20 (Goodspeed).